JUDSON PRESS
PUBLISHERS SINCE 1824

for such a time as this

Young Adults on the Future of the Church

Kathryn Mary Lohre, editor

Foreword by Brian D. McLaren

JUDSON PRESS
PUBLISHERS SINCE 1824

Unless otherwise noted, Scriptures are quoted from the New Revised Standard Version of the Bible, copyright © 1989 by the Division of Christian Education of the National Council of the Churches of Christ in the United States of America. Used by permission. All rights reserved.

Interior design by Beth Oberholtzer.
Cover design by Wendy Ronga and Hampton Design Group.
Awet Andemicael, contributor, photo by Allison Shirreffs, www.allison-shirreffs.net.
Photo credit: Brett Nelson/ELCA of Kathryn Lohre

Library of Congress Cataloging-in-Publication Data
Cataloging-in-Publication Data available upon request.

Contact cip@judsonpress.com.

Printed in the U.S.A.
First Edition, 2014.

Contents

PART TWO
Renewing Hope for the Church's Witness Today and into the Future

Foreword

I've never yet had the privilege of meeting Shantha, Awet, Paul, Jaisy, Jennifer, Kathryn, Ian, R. C., Alison, Erinn, and Zachary in person. But through these pages, I have been introduced to eleven bright, emerging Christian leaders whose voices I needed to hear.

When I was a young Christian leader, I was pretty sure that few of my elder Christian siblings would have listened if I had spoken out the way these eleven have done.

The older generation seemed to be happily preoccupied managing a religious enterprise that they had built ... and that I felt quite marginal to. I didn't begrudge them their happiness and focus. I was glad their religious project was suited to their world. The problem was that I felt I lived in a different world.

As a result, I never published a word until I was over the age of forty. But I remember making a mental note to myself that when I moved into the second half of life, I should be sure to listen to those who were early in the first half.

Listening to the voices of our young people makes sense in a religious movement founded by a thirty-year-old.

That we who are older listen is important, but *how* we listen is equally important. I can think of four especially unhelpful ways to listen.

Sometimes, we older listeners put on patronizing or minimizing filters, praising the "youthful idealism" of our younger colleagues. This faux compliment too easily masks the assumption that, in another ten, twenty, or forty years, they'll be as uncreative and complacent as the rest of us are now!

Sometimes, we older listeners put on cynical and bitter filters: "I used to have big dreams and high ideals too. Let's see how far that gets them." It's as if their potential success in pursuing their dreams would render our lives of less value, so we need to knock them down a peg or two.

Sometimes, we listen through the filters of insult and offense: "What? They're saying the tradition that we faithfully received and passed on isn't good enough for them?" We bristle to imagine they presume the right to revise our historic faith to suit their twenty-first century tastes (forgetting that each generation has adapted and interpreted that same faith throughout history).

Perhaps most unhelpful of all is to listen, all the while thinking, "Good! This will help us appeal to younger people and bring them back to the institutions we have devoted our lives to." Such an approach sees the young as little more than fuel to keep the engines of the religious industrial complex running smoothly for another generation.

Far better to listen with open minds and hearts, realizing that young leaders are not simply leaders of the church of tomorrow. They are leaders of the church of today. They stand alongside the young man Jesus and the young man Timothy, alongside Francis (who began ministry before age 25) and Clare (who became Francis's colleague at age 18) and Calvin (who wrote *The Institutes of the Christian Religion* between ages 19 and 25).

These are voices in a faith movement in which young leaders are meant to be normative.

What does that mean for the rest of us, for whom "young" is receding in life's rear-view mirror at a constant, unstoppable speed?

It means we can't listen merely to patronize, minimize, criticize, or utilize them ... but rather to support, encourage, and work alongside them, envisioning with them, not an either/or vision—either ours or theirs—but a both/and vision in which *ours* is a joint, intergenerational creation.

So, I hope you'll pray to hear what the Spirit is saying to the churches through the voices of Shantha, Awet, Paul, Jaisy, Jennifer, Kathryn, Ian, R. C., Alison, Erinn, and Zachary. God has prepared them for such a time as this. May we have ears to hear.

Brian D. McLaren
speaker/blogger/activist/author
www.brianmclaren.net

Preface

"For Just Such a Time as This": Young Adults and the Future of the Church

KATHRYN MARY LOHRE

Timing Is Everything

I was thirty-four when I began my two-year term as president of the National Council of the Churches of Christ in the USA (NCC), the youngest woman to serve in the role. My nomination had been a surprise, not least of all to me. There were many who saw the writing on the wall and felt that it was time for the Council to be led by a younger person, one who had come of age in our rapidly changing religious landscape. There were others who pointed to my relative youth and outsider status as a major cause for concern, if not an unmitigated risk. The news of my election was met with what I would describe as skeptical hope and latent anxiety about the unknown future I represented.

It was 2012, and the churches were grappling with unprecedented change. As Evangelical, Pentecostal, and ethnic churches were reporting steady growth, the mainline Protestant denominations were in decline. Across the board, financial challenges accelerated by the 2008 financial crisis were amplified by the emergence of new church-dividing issues—human sexuality among them—taking a toll on membership, and in some cases leading to splinter.[1] Globalization and the digital revolution were pushing the boundaries on institutional life, offering the promise of more "nimble" organizations, whatever that means. Social media—and its stunningly effective use in global change movements (think Arab Spring)— were raising expectations for the potential of the churches in the twenty-first century. It was a perfect storm of opportunity—and scary as hell.

A Rapidly Changing Religious Landscape

It's not that the churches aren't accustomed to change. Much of the New Testament documents the transformative changes that took place in the early church. To say nothing of previous millennia, the last century has been a period of the most radical, rapid demographic changes in religious history. The locus of Christianity had shifted from Europe and North America to Africa, Asia, and Latin America, giving rise to new cultural forms and practices and bringing Christianity into increased contact with the world's religions.[2] Global migration patterns and changes to US immigration policies in the mid-1960s put the United States on the fast-track to becoming the most religiously diverse nation on earth, reflecting the spectrum of the world's religions and the diversity of global Christianity.[3]

The years since 9/11 have been monumental in their own right. As Islamophobia reared its ugly head in the United States and around the globe, the desire to reach out to Muslims and to better understand Islam led to the exponential growth of the already burgeoning interfaith movement. This created new possibilities for education and collaboration across faith lines in general and important opportunities for Christian-Muslim dialogue in particular. The increase in interfaith marriages and families and the growth of what is referred to as "multiple religious belonging"— when one person self-identifies with more than one religious tradition or practice—are just beginning to be explored.[4] Campuses, communities, and cities have fast become loci for interreligious engagement, and women, youth, and laypeople are often leading the way.[5] It is clear that the churches' approach to this critical area of work, at all levels, is in dire need of expansion.

Today the majority of people in the United States self-identify as Christian.[6] Yet the statistics are changing as rapidly as the landscape. In 2012 the Pew Forum released a study titled "The Rise of the 'Nones.'" The central finding was that fully one-fifth of the US public—and a third of adults under the age of thirty—are religiously unaffiliated.[7] Many of our churches have understandably become fixated on this data because it points to an impending reality: that within a relatively short period of time, perhaps a single generation, the role of Christianity as the majority religion in the United States will slip if not fall completely. The threat to the churches, it seems, is not religious plurality as it is often claimed, but a waning interest in institutional religion itself.

Discerning Our Common Future

This is the world in which I have come of age—at least in my most formative years. But more importantly, it is the only world in which Millennials—young adults born after 1980—have ever known. Generational studies have given the churches a window into the unknown future, to be sure, but they have also served to strengthen the generational divide. In 2012 the *Yearbook of American & Canadian Churches* published a study titled "Can the Church Log In with the 'Connected Generation'?" The link was made all too directly between the urgent need to reverse the churches' membership decline and the untapped potential of young adults. The strategy offered was for the church to "recalibrat[e] its ministry and mission to meet the needs, and quicken the commitment of Millennials to religious institutions."[8]

I couldn't agree more with the first part of this strategy, but I reject the second. The supersized church institutions of a bygone era have become impossible for any generation to sustain. Why? In short, the role of the churches in American public life simply isn't what it used to be. As a result, the very assumptions on which such institutions were built must now be called into question. The challenge before us, I believe, is not to create new assumptions about our context for Christian witness but to change our posture toward that context. The churches will need to learn new roles as conveners and bridge builders in an era marked by the free exchange of ideas and information through local, national, and global networks.

The churches don't need to be about "hooking" younger generations into the church so that it can return to a past that no longer exists, but about engaging across generations to shape missional goals for the future to which God is calling us. No matter our ages, our hope as Christians is not a hope for our institutions but a hope for the church—a living, growing community called to share the Good News with the world of what God has accomplished in Jesus Christ. The younger among us have more to say and do than to fulfill a demographic void. We want to work on behalf of the least, the last, and the lost. We want to act to overcome the urgent social issues of our time: dire poverty and racism, the devastation of creation, and obscene violence and war. We want to be effective witnesses in today's world, tending to the scandalous divisions within the body of Christ and the scandalous realities of our broken world. I guarantee you that where this is the focus of the churches, the young people will be there. We are already here.

The churches would do well to embrace an abundance mindset: it is no small fact that the majority of young people in the United States self-identify as Christian.[9] This collection seeks to provide an authentic forum for some of our voices. But this project is more than a collection; it is an invitation to intergenerational dialogue: How might we, together, discern the future to which God is calling us as Christians of all ages? Our hope is that there will be a mutual exchange of ideas, experiences, and insights resulting in fresh wisdom, fresh thinking, and fresh ideas for the churches in the twenty-first century.

Accepting the Invitation

Soon after my election as NCC president-elect, I began to feel the heavy burden of others' expectations. How could I possibly represent a younger generation? In 2010 I put out a call for submissions to young adult Christians for their visions for the future of the church. I wanted, in dialogue with my peers, to shape a conversation—rather than to provide a singular, definite narrative. In less than three months, I received almost fifty submissions on a range of topics. I have used these visions to inspire, shape, and engage in dialogue about the future in the contexts where I am privileged to lead. These visions have, in turn, inspired and shaped me.

I selected the essays in this collection with the intention of balancing not only the themes discussed but also a variety of male and female voices, representing a range of churches and perspectives, though the collection is still very limited in these categories. This work, as it stands, remains unfinished; the breadth of Christian diversity in the United States is grossly underrepresented here, as is the depth of Christian perspective. Further, the very fact that the scope of this project is limited to the United States presents its own shortcomings, as we are all now global citizens. We welcome your participation in this dialogue in order to expand and enhance the limited vision provided here.

Each essay is solely the work of its author, without endorsement from any church body or institution. I do not personally subscribe to all of the opinions and perspectives presented in this collection, but I am confident that the content of these essays will encourage authentic dialogue about the future to which God is calling us. To facilitate this purpose, each author has framed practical discussion questions, which you are encouraged to adapt to best suit your context and needs.

The collection is organized into two sections. The first, "Re-envisioning Christian Identity and Relationships," offers new perspectives on what it means to be Christian today—including how we relate to other Christians and people of other traditions.

Shantha Ready Alonso explores how interracial and interethnic identities provide a window into understanding today's multicultural church. R. C. Miessler shares what it means to be spiritual *and* religious, to engage with a variety of Christian traditions from an Orthodox perspective. Jaisy Joseph uncovers the unique challenges of second-generation immigrant Christians and looks anew at Jesus Christ as a model for hope. Jennifer T. Lancaster presents the new reality of global Christianities in the United States and the unique opportunities facing Protestant churches in relationship to and with immigrant congregations. Paul David Brown suggests the potential of the local context for uniting Christians in faith and service to the world. Awet Andemicael makes a biblically grounded case for Christian participation in interfaith dialogue in today's multireligious world.

The second section, "Renewing Hope for the Church's Witness Today and into the Future," invites the reader to look through different lenses to see new possibilities for Christian witness in a rapidly changing context. Ian S. Mevorach challenges the churches to address the intersection between the climate crisis and racism, or eco-racism. Erinn Staley offers hope for the churches' full inclusion of people with intellectual disabilities and all those who are excluded. Jennifer S. Leath calls for ministries that tend to the whole person, including sexual identity, from the particular context of the black church traditions. Alison VanBuskirk Philip offers two compelling women-led models for listening in Christian community that lead to personal, communal, and global transformation. Zachary Ugolnik urges the churches in the digital era to cultivate face-to-face rituals and experiences for women and men to be overwhelmed by divine beauty.

Regardless of how you approach the content, we hope that you will do so with others, preferably a mixed-generation group. The most meaningful Christian formation I have received has been through intergenerational dialogue, or mutual mentoring. It has changed my life, helped me to clarify my calling, and given me assurance that there is indeed a place for me in the church—not as a young person, but as a child of God. In my own vision for the future, mutual mentoring will enable us to be responsible to our legacy as churches and responsive to the ever-changing context in which we witness to Christ. In this spirit, we offer in dialogue our hopes, dreams, and visions for the future, inviting the Holy Spirit to lead us as we move forward together. Thanks be to God for all that is yet unknown, and for calling us—the likes of Esther and Aaron—to speak, to lead, and to prophesy the future of the church "for just such a time as this" (Esther 4:14).

DISCUSSION QUESTIONS

1. How might we think about the renewal of the church today?

2. What criteria, other than membership and money, can we use to measure the growth and impact of the church?

3. How might digital technologies be used effectively in the formation of authentic Christian communities? How have you experienced Christian community online?

4. What are some examples of intergenerational work in your church? What are the best practices? Where is there room for growth?

5. What is your vision for the future of the church?

NOTES

1. For example, the 2009 adoption of the social statement, "Human Sexuality, Gift and Trust," by the Evangelical Lutheran Church in America was a primary factor in the formation of the North American Lutheran Church the following year.

2. Todd M. Johnson and Kenneth R. Ross, *Atlas of Global Christianity* (Edinburgh: Edinburgh University Press, 2010).

3. Diana L. Eck, *A New Religious America: How a "Christian Country" Has Become the World's Most Religiously Diverse Nation* (New York: Harper Collins, 2001).

4. Catherine Cornille, *Many Mansions? Multiple Religious Belonging and Christian Identity* (Maryknoll, NY: Orbis, 2002).

5. "America's Interfaith Infrastructure: A Pilot Study," *The Pluralism Project at Harvard University*, accessed April 23, 2013, http://www.pluralism.org/interfaith.

6. "US Religious Landscape Survey, Religious Beliefs and Practices: Diverse and Politically Relevant," *The Pew Forum on Religion and Public Life*, June 2008, accessed April 23, 2013, http://religions.pewforum.org/pdf/report2-religious-landscape-study-full.pdf, 8. As of 2008, Christians accounted for 78.4 percent of the total population, whereas all other religious traditions together accounted for 4.7 percent.

7. "'Nones' on the Rise," *The Pew Forum on Religion and Public Life*, October 9, 2012, accessed April 23, 2013, http://www.pewforum.org/Unaffiliated/nones-on-the-rise.aspx.

8. Eileen W. Lindner, "Can the Church Log In with the 'Connected Generation?'" in *Yearbook of American & Canadian Churches 2012*, ed. Eileen W. Lindner (Nashville: Abingdon, 2012), 19.

9. "Religion among the Millennials," *The Pew Forum on Religion and Public Life*, February 17, 2010, accessed April 23, 2013, http://www.pewforum.org/Age/Religion-Among-the-Millennials.aspx, 3.

Acknowledgments

I owe a debt of gratitude to so many who have supported this project over the past four years. Several friends and colleagues in the National Council of the Churches of Christ in the USA (NCC) encouraged this idea from the very beginning. I am deeply indebted to A. Roy Medley, general secretary of the American Baptist Churches USA, and to Judson Press for making the commitment with me to bring it to life in the form of this book.

I have been blessed to have several vocational mentors in the church over the years who have helped me to envision the future to which God is calling us, and to discern the role I am called to play. Those people include Jean and Dan Martensen, Joanne Chadwick, Ann Tiemeyer, Diana Eck, Donald J. McCoid, and Mark S. Hanson.

My parents, Mary and John Lohre, have offered a lifetime of encouragement, love, and support, always reminding me whose I am. Most of all, I am grateful to my loving husband, Tim Seitz, my partner in ministry, family, and life, and to our three children, John, Benjamin, and Hannah. Thank you for daily grounding me in what matters most.

To the essayists featured here, and to all others whose submissions shaped this work, my heartfelt gratitude. You have given me hope beyond measure, and I am eager to share this hope with others in the churches. I truly believe that all of you are called as leaders for the future of the church "for just such a time as this" (Esther 4:14). For this, I give thanks to God!

PART ONE

Reenvisioning Christian Identity and Relationships

CHAPTER 1

What Are You?

Hybrid Identities and Today's Multicultural Church

SHANTHA READY ALONSO

"What are you?" a stranger asked as I stood in line at a pit stop McDonald's in Iowa. I was a living enigma that didn't fit the racial-ethnic categories familiar to him. I could not tell if his question was hostile, curious, or both. Lowering my eyes, I said nothing, blinking back hot tears while I waited in line for the strawberry milkshake I no longer desired.

Years later this encounter continues to haunt me. What am I? Well, I am the daughter of a fourth-generation Irish American Roman Catholic father and a first-generation Indian American raised-Lutheran/spiritual-explorer mother. I was baptized Roman Catholic and raised in the Washington, DC metro area. I married a Mexican American man from California. Sometimes I have fun trying to pass as a Latin@[1] when I speak a little Spanish and dance *salsa*. But that's where I came from and who I married and how others see me. *What am I?* I'm part this and part that, and all the parts influence who I am. Today's lexicon lacks one clear answer that speaks for the whole me.

In many ways, my individual experience is a microcosm of a demographic shift happening in churches across the United States. Once many people took pride in being Syrian Orthodox, Norwegian Lutheran, or Irish Catholic—denomination was deeply tied to ethnicity. Now we're all dropping out, switching, and mixing. Some would call what's happening an identity crisis in the church. In academia they might say this change is part of the *postmodern landscape* our churches don't know how to manage. Unprecedented multicultural mixing has broken open paradigms of difference once seen as ultimate truths. Whatever we call this change, it is time to stop peering into the faces of our churches' people and seeing enigmas. These changes are bringing God's gifts to the church in new ways.

Gift 1: Living into Our Hybrid Identities

God has gifted humankind with a powerful love. Love overcomes barriers of fear and division. Love makes us remember that we are all interdependent parts in the one body of God. Pope John Paul II summed up in *Ut Unum Sint* what has proven true for millennials (and our parents) in many ways: "Love is the great undercurrent which gives life and adds vigor to the movement towards unity."[2] The great undercurrent of love is pushing us toward a generational shift in our homes, our communities, and the churches. I credit the great undercurrent of love in my identity formation process. I am one of many children of the millennial generation born to courageous parents who intermarried in the face of social taboos, blatant discrimination, and even legal restrictions. Over time those restrictions have weakened and the tide of global migration has risen. The trend of racial-ethnic intermarriage is ever increasing.[3]

Having grown up with people who are different from us, our generation overwhelmingly sees interracial marriage as a positive thing. With 3.2 percent of us reporting being of mixed racial heritage—the most racially and ethnically diverse cohort of youth in the nation's history—hybrid identities have cropped up in the United States.[4] As race and ethnicity are often tied to religion, a lot of interdenominational and interreligious marriages are happening as well. For example, statistics kept by the Greek Orthodox archdiocese indicate that 66 percent of all marriages performed in Greek Orthodox churches are inter-Christian, and overall Greek Orthodox marrying-out trends are estimated to be closer to 75–80 percent.[5] Although most churches do not keep it on record, many Christians now identify with multiple denominations.

Mexican-American theologian Virgilio Elizondo offers a concept I find helpful for understanding what is happening with racial-ethnic and religious blending and blended people in US churches today: *mestizaje*.[6] Elizondo defines *mestizaje* as "the generation of a new people from two disparate parent peoples."[7] *Mestizaje* is not a new phenomenon. On the contrary, over the centuries of human existence, the mixing of peoples has made us a stronger species. The "purest" peoples who do not have exchange with outsiders tend to weaken and die out.

As the breadth and depth of our diversity ever accelerates, more and more of us embody multiple heritages and traditions in a *mestizo* fashion. We are a generation heavily influenced by the great undercurrent of love that broke down the barriers of our parents' and grandparents' generations. It has made us a generation of natural bridge builders and reconcilers. Millennials' hybrid identities and increasing rates of intermarriage have made us more open to diversity than ever and less tolerant of intolerance. We refuse to be divided against ourselves, as we increasingly embody creative combinations of the radical diversity that is the body of Christ. We embrace the gifts of unity we see in our local communities, and we recognize a need for those realities to be made manifest in divided churches.

Gift 2: Reframing the Tension between Unity and Diversity

Cultivating a healthy tension between unity and diversity is a practice churches have engaged generation after generation, and sure enough, millennials are remixing it once again for our time. As the gospel spread across the world, it had to be interpreted and inculturated in many ways. Over the centuries, the church has been resilient by interpreting the gifts of diverse cultures, embracing them in unity with one another and in keeping with the gospel. This is also the history of the movement for Christian unity among different Christian traditions, starting with the Council of Nicea into the present day. Unity could not mean sameness, or the churches would be irrelevant in different cultures. Diversity could not mean separation, as that would undermine the Christian call to build community and walk together in our journey to live the gospel.

Calls for unity among people of diverse backgrounds can cause anxiety that a unique theology, tradition, or culture will fade away into an amorphous, boring sameness. Some worry that the dominant traditions will win while the smaller ones get swallowed up into extinction—or, the lowest common denominator will become our highest aspiration. Yet the reality is that without interacting and learning from different church traditions, isolated traditions will become increasingly irrelevant. Rather than creating sameness, encounters of difference create *mestizaje*: sharpened self-awareness, cultural critique, and creative new thinking.

Awakening to the tension inherent in living out unity and diversity can be troubling for people of mixed heritage. Although my family background is quite ecumenical (coming from many different Christian traditions), in all my fourteen years of Roman Catholic education, as well as going to church and praying with my family members of different Protestant, Orthodox, and Catholic denominations, I never thought of our unity as a family amid our diversity of Christian traditions as *a gift*. If anything, it was sometimes very interesting and other times an annoying inconvenience.

During high school, as I studied the sacraments, the words "This is my body, given up for you," took on a whole new meaning for me. I began to realize that there was something deeply wrong with the fact that at Communion time every Sunday at our family's Roman Catholic church, I would squeeze through the narrow pew and step over my own mother as I made the journey down the aisle to receive the Eucharist while she stayed behind. I came to appreciate the faithful sacrifices my mother made to raise my sister and me—her body, given up for us. Yet her Christian faith, formed in its own fusion of Mar Thoma, Church of South India,[8] and Iowan Lutheran traditions, was not welcome at the Catholic Communion table.

Over the years, this has become a great paradox to me. On the one hand, I crave to be in community with my fellow Roman Catholics and enter into the mysterious and powerful Eucharist, tasting the already-but-not-yet deep transformation of our communities into unity with Christ, into God's wholeness, God's *shalom*. On the other hand, my mother and others with whom I share lived experiences of Christ's love are not allowed to come to the Communion table. If I was in my mother's womb sharing lifeblood, memories, and hopes with her for a lifetime, shouldn't I be able to share the Eucharist with her? For a long time, I stopped taking Communion altogether. Even now I do not commune when I am attending Catholic Mass with a Christian who is not welcome at the table.

Many young people gather around the rallying cry of building a more inclusive church that accepts people of different identities. Much of this desire for more inclusiveness comes from their lived experiences of *mestizaje*. As more people of mixed traditions form families and build community, our churches will need to listen to and be led by more people who live out *mestizo* experiences. If our churches are going to evolve and bring new generations in, they must reflect changes in society—they must reflect who we are.

Gift 3: Putting Our Energy Where It Will Make a Difference

On a trip home from college, I expressed my frustration about the exclusive practices of the Roman Catholic Communion table and my desire to change it to a family member. With compassionate eyes and a gentle hand on my shoulder, he told me the church is not a democracy, and I should put my energy and gifts where they will make a difference. It turns out I am not alone in heeding this advice. In my work with young adult Christians, I have gained some insight into what does and does not motivate my peers to engage in church. My overall assessment is this: we go where we believe our energy and gifts will make a difference.

Millennials are known for identifying as "spiritual but not religious," and our loyalty to church institutions is notoriously weak. Denominational policies and statements held more authority in a time when people desired to be represented by or spoken for—it was easier to be represented or spoken for when there was more homogeneity in the denominations. In a time when our opinions and identities are more diverse than ever and we have technology to be in direct communication, we gravitate toward opportunities that honor individuals' agency to be proactive in networking, dialoguing, and growing in faith together.

Many have become disillusioned with denominational infighting, mismanaged sex abuse scandals, institutional self-protection at the expense of mission, and perhaps most importantly, fear of the other (religious, racial/ethnic, gender, and sexual orientation). We do not share the anxieties of our parents' and grandparents' generations about denominational divisions or institutional decline, as many of us perceive old institutions to be quite broken. Instead of going to churches where we have to sort out these complicated and often discouraging matters, I see my peers putting their energy elsewhere. Millennials are known for idealism and volunteerism. Millennials hunger to understand our own heritages and to deeply encounter other cultures. We're often doing it in different places than traditional church structures. We pour energy into projects with faith-based and civic organizations with specific missions that offer ways to develop leadership gifts, build community, nourish spirituality, and bring needed service and social change to our communities.

These same qualities that millennials are drawn to are qualities the church has offered communities before and must continue to provide as an agent of God's mission. I do not fear that God's church will fail to manifest itself in the world. The gospel and the community that gathers to live it out are too strong to die. Yet, due to some of the challenges listed above, Millennials lack a sense of continuity with the institutional manifestations of church that have gone before us. A great heritage is being lost. The generational disconnect in the church is extreme in the US context. Millennials, if invited, have spiritual gifts to bridge divides, foster dialogue, and connect to that heritage. To do so, denominations must be ready to consider the new perspectives that come with the gifts and energy of new members and leaders.

Gift 4: Scaring the Parents

Let's be real. The changes happening in the religious landscape right now scare a lot of people who are invested in institutions crafted in a time when blended and blending people were not a major influence. New identities disrupt the old traditions and structures. I love one challenge a group of religious mestizo teens sent their parents at the 2003 Association of Interchurch Families in Rome: "It is not we who are confused in refusing to choose one church or the other. It is you of former generations who have been confused in accepting and perpetuating the divisions of the churches. Christ willed only one church."[9] Theologian Virgilio Elizondo unpacks why such challenges can feel scary:

> A *mestizo* group represents a particularly serious threat to its two parent cultures. The *mestizo* does not fit conveniently into the analysis categories used by either parent group. The *mestizo* may understand them far better than they understand him or her. To be an insider-outsider, as is the *mestizo*—is to have closeness to and distance from both parent cultures. A *mestizo* people can see and appreciate characteristics in its parent cultures that they see neither in themselves nor in each other.[10]

Interchurch families know what this Christian *mestizaje* means on a practical, lived level. Family rituals are one vehicle for living out *mestizaje* together. I'll offer death rituals in my family as an example. At my maternal grandfather's deathbed, we made a circle around him and sang "How Great Thou Art," followed by a hymn in his native Malayalam. Meanwhile, it was comforting to my paternal grandmother to have the Eucharist brought to her. After a death in my husband's family, we prayed the whole rosary in Spanish together in a chapel.

After having all these powerful experiences, at the age of thirty I can imagine myself, God willing, an old woman having lived a full life. I am on my deathbed receiving the Eucharist, then listening to family members circled around me singing "How Great Thou Art." I am whispering to my loved ones to ask them one more time if they have old programs from family members' funerals so they can integrate a Spanish rosary and a few words of Malayalam into a hymn, to honor those who went before me. This is how I envision creative fusion of my families' cultures, traditions, and languages playing out in my life. If this is what I want, I suspect my children will grow up expecting to become architects of language, tradition, and culture to fit their own contexts and experiences. They'll be part me and part my husband and part where and how they were raised. Maybe they'll interpret their contexts and realities in ways that will scare me!

The Challenge: Accepting God's Gifts

Are people who embody a Christian *mestizaje* bold enough to seek out all generations of the church and work through the lack of understanding and potential pain of rejection by those who are scared of them? Or, will the trend continue that young people simply opt out of formal church settings and seek another spiritual community that is open to new hybrid identities? I don't have answers, but I do have hope.

First, I hope that if and when a stranger ever again asks me or anyone like me, *"What are you?"* we will have learned from our church and communities to just laugh out loud and say, "Silly, I'm a human being made in the image of God!" (I've had sixteen years to think about that one.) Furthermore, I'd continue to elaborate by explaining I'm a woman who honors my roots by embracing and practicing many life-giving traditions I have learned from my family. I critique my parent cultures by helping ugly practices of exclusion die out with my generation and by advocating for systems of inclusivity. Creative tensions between my identities quiver and pull on the strands of my DNA. The friction pumps a restless and holy energy through my veins to reconcile the paradox of wanting *both* unity for inclusive communities *and* liberation for diverse and too-often marginalized identities. There are many like me who are ready to bring God's gifts of a *mestizo* mind-set to God's church.

Second, I have hope that a *mestizo* mind-set will be taken seriously, and therefore people with blended identities will not opt out of a confining church where repression of one part of an identity or another is required. By extension, I hope more churches will fully recognize the church around the block or on the other side of town as a valid and beautiful expression of God's diverse manifestations of community in mission. Getting to that level of respect and understanding will require studying and understanding the cultural riches of our traditions while also being proactive in naming and ending any ignorance, imperialism, persecution, pride, grudges, or racism that might have once divided us. The great undercurrent of love is moving us into a new opportunity to receive God's gift of unity. All we have to do is accept it and share it with others.

DISCUSSION QUESTIONS

1. What are some of the hybrid identities you observe in your community? How might these identities be better embraced as God's gifts?

2. Have you ever had an experience of discrimination? How did that shape you? How does your faith inform your understanding of who you are?

3. Are there places of exclusion in your church? What can you do to make them more inclusive?

4. What are some cultural shifts you see taking place in the changing religious landscape that scare you? Why are they scary? How can this fear be overcome?

5. What are some of God's gifts that you can identify emerging in your own life? In your community? In your church? How can these be celebrated?

NOTES

1. *Latin@* is a coined term that serves as a gender-inclusive description of Latino/Latina identity. It is pronounced *la-TEE-no-ah*.

2. Pope John Paul II, *Ut Unum Sint: Our Commitment to Ecumenism* (Rome: Second Vatican Ecumenical Council, 1995), accessed April 23, 2013, http://www.vatican.va/holy_father/john_paul_ii/encyclicals/documents/hf_jp-ii_enc_25051995_ut-unum-sint_en.html.

3. "A record 14.6 percent of all new marriages in the United States in 2008 were between spouses of a different race or ethnicity from each other, according to a Pew Research Center analysis of new data from the U.S. Census Bureau. That figure is an estimated six times the intermarriage rate among newlyweds in 1960 and more than double the rate in 1980." Jeffery Passel, Wendy Wang, Paul Taylor, "One-in-Seven New U.S. Marriages Is Interracial or Interethnic: Marrying Out," *Pew Research Center—Social and Demographic Trends*, June 4, 2010, accessed April 23, 2013, http://www.pewsocialtrends .org/2010/06/04/marrying-out/.

4. "Almost All Millennials Accept Interracial Dating and Marriage," *Pew Research Center*, February 1, 2010, accessed April 23, 2013, http://www .pewresearch.org/2010/02/01/almost-all-millennials-accept-interracial-dating-and-marriage/.

5. Lewis J. Patsovos and Charles L. Joanides, "Interchurch Marriages: An Orthodox Perspective," *International Academy for Marital Spirituality Review* 6 (2000): 215–23, http://www.goarch.org/archdiocese/departments/marriage/ interfaith/journal-articles-1/documents/patsavos-joanides-article.pdf.

6. The term *mestizaje* has historically been used to refer specifically to the mixing of Spanish and Native American indigenous peoples, the result of the Spanish-American War and colonial domination tactics. This is not the sense of the word I wish to evoke. Elizondo takes a holistic view of the term *mestizaje*, using the *mestizo* experience to refer to the embodiment of multiple cultures in one person. He takes a strengths-based approach to understanding the significance of this mixing experience, using a Mexican-American lens.

7. Virgilio Elizondo, *Galilean Journey: The Mexican-American Promise* (Maryknoll, NY: Orbis, 1983), 16.

8. My grandmother married into the Mar Thoma Syrian Christian Church, which traces its roots in Kerala, India, to the first century, attributing its founding to the evangelism of St. Thomas. My grandmother's family had always been very involved in the Church of South India. Seven generations before my grandmother, an ancestor had translated the Bible from English into her family's native language, Malayalam. Intermarriage between the Mar Thoma and Church of South India traditions was accepted at the time my grandparents married. They married in the church of my grandmother's childhood, while she agreed to raise their children in the Mar Thoma tradition. Little did she know that she and my grandfather would move to the midwestern United States and receive hospitality from Lutherans. You can learn more about the Mar Thoma Church at marthoma.org and about the Church of South India at http://www.csisynod.com/.

9. "Interchurch Families and Christian Unity: Rome 2003," Association of Interchurch Families, (2003), 4, accessed April 23, 2013, http://interchurchfamilies.org/confer/rome2003/documents/roma2003_en.pdf.

10. Elizondo, *Galilean Journey*, 18.

CHAPTER 2

Piecing It Together

Spiritual Tinkering from an Orthodox Perspective

R. C. MIESSLER

Lego as Spiritual Metaphor

As a quiet, introverted kid, Legos were my favorite toys. I could create, change, and end entire worlds in an afternoon. When getting a new set, I always created what the instructions intended. After a few days of play, however, I would explore new configurations, adding in bricks from other sets. In recent years, I have started collecting Legos again, and the complexity of the sets today is astounding. Even so, the underlying concept is still there: the pieces are universal, interlock with each other, and can easily be taken apart. I can take the Lego sets I have acquired in the last few years and mix them up with my childhood collection, and everything will fit together.

The Lego philosophy is an appropriate metaphor for my spiritual journey. I was born to a Methodist mother and Episcopalian father, and spent most of my formative years in very conservative independent nondenominational Christian churches. After taking a church history class in college, I began to explore the Eastern

Orthodox Church, and I was received as a convert in 2003.[1] Several years later, I attended a liberal Christian Church (Disciples of Christ) seminary, where I studied ecumenism and desired to find a way to form bridges between evangelical Protestant and Eastern Orthodox Christians. In recent years, I have grown fond of the worship and social action of The Episcopal Church.

I admire cradle-to-grave Christians, but I am a spiritual tinkerer, and in this I am not alone. More and more religious people are becoming spiritual tinkerers, piecing together a spirituality that makes sense to them. Some of us have no permanent church home—others are happily rooted in a tradition yet bring in pieces from other traditions. As an Eastern Orthodox Christian, I am a member of a church that considers itself to be "one, holy, catholic, and apostolic"; and as a spiritual tinkerer, I believe there is much to be gained from both tradition and creative engagement with other practices.

Changes in the Church

Today institutional religion is losing influence. The Pew Forum's research on religious affiliation showed that in 2012 nearly 20 percent of U.S. adults considered themselves unaffiliated with any religious tradition.[2] While this group, labeled the "nones" or "unaffiliated," includes around six percent who identify as atheist and agnostic, it also includes those who consider themselves religious or spiritual—though only 10 percent are actively looking for an organized religious group to join. Of significance as well is that almost one-third of 18 to 29-year-olds consider themselves unaffiliated, the largest percentage of any age group.[3] Those in the United States, and increasingly younger Americans, are moving away from the religious structures that dominated the twentieth century, seeking spiritual insight outside of religious institutions.

Protestant denominations have been quick to raise questions about how to adapt to today's rapidly changing religious landscape. At the same time, however, some Christians are more concerned about maintaining the traditions of their faith, which often include institutional structures. The Eastern Orthodox Church is one such tradition. Orthodoxy places emphasis on the idea of apostolic succession—that all clergy have been ordained in an unbroken line since Jesus chose the apostles. Therefore, the institution and structure of the Orthodox Church is a matter of theology and cannot easily be changed. This creates tension between the urge of Orthodox Christians to retreat into a structured, institutional faith and the general shift among many other American Christians to push back against their institutions as imperfect, impermanent constructs that can and should be reformed.

In 2011 Alexei Krindatch, an Orthodox sociologist, published the first census of Orthodox Christians in the United States. It is a comprehensive look at the demographics and beliefs of Orthodox Christians in America, including attitudes about changes in the faith and perceptions of the future of Orthodoxy in the United States. The census indicates nearly two-thirds of the laity believe that the clergy must uphold the traditions of the Orthodox faith without deviation, while the rest feel that priests must be open to change and adapt Orthodox traditions. Out of the laity who considered themselves to be moderate or liberal, however, 74 percent believe clergy must be open to change.[4] The survey of the laity also indicates that 21 percent feel that Orthodox Christians are too tied to the past, and 29 percent believe the church is making good steps toward change and progress.[5] Only 16 percent feel that parishes should explore new forms and patterns of liturgical life, and 19 percent agreed that individual Orthodox Christians should be free to interpret Scripture and tradition on their own, and to tolerate the interpretations of others.[6]

Orthodox Christians are increasingly concerned about the relationship between American culture and the traditions and practices of the Orthodox Church.[7] Interestingly, older Orthodox Christians were found to be more in favor of open interpretation and toleration, while younger Orthodox are more interested in maintaining traditional beliefs, believing that the Orthodox Church needs to look to the past and return to traditional beliefs and practices.[8] This was not the result expected by the census, as it was hypothesized that the younger faithful would be more in favor of change. In general, other religious youth tend to be more experimental, with a more irreverent attitude toward tradition and a willingness to tinker, or to bring seemingly disparate parts of various spiritual traditions together into a form that helps them make sense of their spiritual journeys. While Orthodox youth may be more inclined toward a conservative approach toward their faith, other Christians are more likely to tinker and experiment, using Orthodox Christianity as inspiration; therefore, Orthodox Christians need to be aware of the nature of religious tinkering so they can understand why other Christians are drawn to their faith without officially converting to Orthodoxy.

Spiritual Tinkering

Sociologist Robert Wuthnow describes the approach that many young adults take to religion as "tinkering."[9] They take what they need from culture, utilizing whatever resources they need to create sense out of the uncertainties of life. Improvisation and drawing from the experiences of others become the norm for problem solving.[10] Wuthnow writes, "Ordinary people are not religious professionals who approach spirituality the way an engineer might construct a building. They are amateurs who make do with what they can."[11] If young adults are having less exposure to organized religion as they grow up, the path that religion can often provide is less defined than it was for their parents.

Wuthnow does not want to characterize all young adults as tinkerers; people of all ages are tinkerers, and some do not participate in spiritual tinkering at all.[12] However, he does feel that the "typical" young adult today participates in religious tinkering. The extent of tinkering varies. Some young adults may, for example, believe traditional Christian doctrines, yet they do not participate in a traditional worship experience on Sunday morning or even belong to a church. Wuthnow writes, "The core holds steady, persuading one that the Bible is still a valuable source of moral insight, for example, but the core is amended almost continuously through conversations with friends, reflections about an especially meaningful experience on vacation or at work, or from a popular song."[13] It is not enough to encounter God in church for an hour on Sunday morning, but to find God in anything that inspires them. To support this, tinkerers have used the Internet to create virtual, grassroots religious and spiritual congregations, where people can form communities and discuss the issues that impact them.

The danger of tinkering can be found in its lack of context. Piecing together various religious doctrines and practices may remove them from their intended place in history and space. However, it can also serve to reinvent these concepts or introduce them to people who may never have been exposed to them in the first place. It is important, therefore, for the tinkerer to remain connected to the past and conscious of the context out of which the various doctrines and practices are plucked. Protestants who draw from concrete components of Orthodox worship, such as candles and icons, and liturgical elements such as prayers and orders of service, have likely been exposed to these elements before, sometimes even in their own traditions.

Shortly after being received into the Orthodox Church, I attended a Methodist service with my parents. During Communion, an icon of Christ was brought out as a focal point. This was one of the first times I had noticed seeing an icon used in Christian worship outside of an Orthodox service, and it was jarring at first. However, it was interesting to see that icons were not something unique to the Orthodox faith, and it gave me one of my first real exposures to how other traditions might use Orthodox spiritual practices to enrich their own discipline. It is rare to find Protestants who attempt to recreate Orthodox worship word for word and action for action. Instead, elements of Orthodox worship are placed alongside contemporary worship bands, interpretive dance, and evangelical preaching and Bible teaching. In this sense, these Christians are truly attempting a universal experience by drawing from the traditions of the entire church throughout time and space. Orthodox Christians do not have a monopoly on their worship practices and theological viewpoints—they belong to the entire church, and the tinkerers understand this.

Theologian Leonard Sweet believes the attraction of younger Protestants to Eastern Orthodoxy is because they want an "interactive, immersive" experience in worship.[14] Christians raised in a media-rich environment are discovering how Orthodox Christianity engages the senses in worship.[15] However, Christian tinkerers may not feel at home in either Protestant or Orthodox churches, so they are creating something that speaks to their ultimate concerns, paying tribute to the beliefs, doctrines, and practices that bring them close to God. If Protestants are drawing from Orthodox practices but not engaging in dialogue with Orthodox Christians, they are missing a chance to be part of a larger conversation, just as Orthodox Christians who refuse to engage in dialogue with Protestants are missing out on understanding what the future of Christian faith might look like. Both sides have a chance to be part of a dialogue, based in the idea of ancient-future Christian faith.

Ancient-Future Christianity

Orthodoxy embodies the ancient faith, providing an experience of Christian mystery, community, and symbol dating back to the Byzantine Empire. I have heard the Orthodox Church described as a "time machine," where worshippers step into a church and are sent back a thousand years. While it is an amazing trip, eventually Christians need to return to the present, and it can be jarring to move between the ancient faith held by the Orthodox and the realities of American society today. Orthodoxy cannot be a "living museum" of Christian faith if it wants to survive, and it must be willing to evolve and change as it engages new cultures, not simply carry on as it always has.[16]

The late theologian Robert Webber's concept of "ancient-future Christianity" attempts to create "a dialogue between the old and the new."[17] I appreciate the concept of ancient-future in my own spiritual life, as it is a convergence of different ways of looking at faith: the ancient is moving into the future, while simultaneously, the future is looking to the past. This way of looking at Christianity does not leave the past behind, nor does it change simply for the sake of doing something new; instead, it is a forward-looking way of faith that is rooted firmly in the past. The ancient Christian practices and doctrine form a foundation for the future of the faith while not remaining stuck in the past, unwilling or unable to change.

Unfortunately, many Christians (not only the Orthodox) are so wedded to a concept of an ancient and unchanging faith that they are failing to address the needs of the faithful today. Other Christians want change to the point that they are willing to give up the past in order to move forward. Both of these extreme approaches are problematic; ancient Christians unwilling to move forward are left behind, and future-facing Christians with no anchor in the past quickly lose momentum. As a spiritual tinkerer, I believe that we can serve as bridge builders between the ancient and the future, probing history in search of the common faith that has been present throughout Christianity in all cultures.

The use of ancient faith practices can act as a stabilizer in times of rapid change. Yet it is not enough for Protestants to reach into Orthodoxy—Orthodox Christians must also reach out to Protestants, seeking dialogue and mutual enrichment. Without this exchange, the risk is that ancient spiritual practices may be appropriated as yet another "gimmick" in an already consumer-driven church model that seeks to get people in the pews (or, as it were, stadium seating). Without serious reflection on the theology behind them, it is possible that a penchant for ancient Christian practices will simply fade away, a fleeting fad.

Orthodox Christian Tinkerers?

Orthodox priest and theologian Alexander Schmemann describes the Orthodox situation in the West as "schizophrenia." Schmemann is convinced that Orthodox Christians are living a double life—that of Eastern Christians on Sunday morning and of Western Americans the rest of the week. This leads them to believe that they are preserving Orthodox traditions, even though they are entrenched in the Protestant ethos of American public life.[18] While Orthodox Christians celebrate the divine liturgy of the East, worship in buildings based on Byzantine architecture, and hold to the teachings of the church fathers, they generally embrace the concepts of pluralism, democracy, and the civic religion of America.

This is not to say that the values of American culture and society are antithetical to Orthodox beliefs, but it does challenge the idea of truth being preserved entirely in the Orthodox Christian faith—that it is indeed the "one, holy, catholic, and apostolic church." Of course, there are many ways to interpret that phrase in the Nicene Creed. The Eastern Orthodox Church could be considered that "one church," with all other Christians in error, or it could be a mystical concept of a unified body of believers that transcends denominational differences. I prefer to believe in the latter, as do other Orthodox Christians, but we are in the vast minority.

Is it really possible to be an Orthodox tinkerer? I believe that many already tinker in some fashion, bringing the occasional element from another Christian tradition—or sometimes another religion entirely—into their daily lives. However, this all seemingly comes to a halt in the narthex on Sunday morning, when the divine liturgy begins. Perhaps most Orthodox Christians—content with ancient worship, beliefs, and practices—are not inclined to become spiritual tinkerers. Yet at the very least, I would urge Orthodox Christians to attend services of other traditions from time to time throughout the year. My own spiritual journey has been richly enhanced by attending Protestant and ecumenical worship services. Recently, I have made it a habit to attend services at an Episcopal church on Christmas Eve. I also draw from contemplative activities of Zen Buddhism and the interpretation of Torah in Judaism. Of course, every tinkerer will have their own sources they will draw from; some of my Orthodox friends have found inspiration in Catholic monasteries, Pentecostal praise music, and Rastafarianism.

The Orthodox may not be tinkerers for the most part, but they do play a role in it, by acting as exemplars of ancient Christian practices and belief. Even if Orthodox Christians are concerned about changes in the church, they can still work with other Christians who are interested in how they can use the ancient faith of the church to enhance their own spiritual journeys. It is charitable, then, for Orthodox Christians to act as mentors and guides, to show other Christians the treasures they hold on to and how to use them responsibly. In this sense, Orthodoxy is the guest at the diverse banquet of these various Christians who let the Orthodox traditions into their lives, not the host who controls every detail and sets the tone. In turn, other Christians should be charitable toward the Orthodox, not expecting them to change to conform to their expectations, taking the gifts that the Orthodox can offer without distorting them, and always acknowledging their source.

Eventually the Orthodox Church is going to have to seriously consider the same issues that have become of vital importance in other churches: ordination of female pastors, the role of LGBT members in the church, an increasing awareness of religious plurality, and the growing demographic of atheists and agnostics. This is not to say Orthodoxy has not discussed these topics, or that all Orthodox Christians hold the same beliefs. The clergy and laity of Orthodoxy cover the gamut, from very conservative to very liberal, much like any other religious tradition. However, if Krindatch's census is any indicator, most Orthodox Christians do not consider these to be negotiable, at least right now, and it is uncharitable to push Orthodoxy to make these issues the primary points of discussion.

The Orthodox Church in the United States has several challenges it needs to overcome in the next few decades. To name one, the question of ethnic identity has to be addressed, as the various national Orthodox jurisdictions in the United States determine what it will take to transform into an American Orthodox Church headed by one patriarch, with a common language for the divine liturgy on Sundays. I am hopeful that this and other issues, such as a common date for Easter, will be addressed in time. However, while I do not advocate pushing the Orthodox Church to the brink of schism in order to bring change, as has happened in some Protestant mainline denominations, I do feel that we need to be more proactive in working to find ways to engage the culture around us.

Lego Christianity and Tinkering

When considering the reality of religious pluralism in the United States, as well as tendencies of youth to engage in spiritual tinkering, my mind returns to the Lego concept to understand the creative ways Christians today express their faith. Traditional Christians have similarities to Lego users who build only the model in the instructions with no deviation. Some more adventurous Christians have set aside the instructions, preferring to mix everything in one giant tub and build new creations of their own. While some Christians may be concerned about the problem of syncretism, or creating a new religion out of seemingly disparate traditions, Christianity has successfully found ways to become relevant to various cultures, absorbing various customs and practices while maintaining its core doctrines.

I doubt that Christian tinkerers are actively seeking to create a new religion or to convert themselves away from Christianity. The foundation of Christian faith is still there, but tinkerers are trying to build on it, just as Lego builders rely on the philosophy that all bricks can connect with each other. If we truly believe that Christianity is a catholic, or universal, faith, then we should not be worried that other religions and spiritual practices will undermine it. Yet Christian tinkerers need to be charitable, as not all Christians have the same views on appropriating practices and beliefs from other traditions. Sometimes the tinkerer needs to respect the spiritual needs or boundaries of others.

Just as my own fascination with Legos has been rekindled in recent years, I have noticed that my generation is a nostalgic one. We search for long-lost toys and fondly remembered television shows. This occurs in other generations as well, but I think this impulse has been amplified in the digital age. Young adults want to maintain this connection to the past by procuring relics that remind us of a simpler time. It is easy to have this same nostalgia for a simpler Christianity, as evidenced by various restoration and primitivism movements that have cropped up over time. In reality, the history of the church is messy, full of dissension, and rarely straightforward. There is, in short, no simpler time to which we can return.

Today, when I look at the Orthodox Church, I see an expression of Christian faith based in the historical context of the medieval Eastern Roman Empire, a tradition that emerged and endured despite schisms, repression, and war. The survival of Orthodoxy is a testament to the faith of millions of Christians who brought their faith through the horrors of genocide and communism. I understand the need felt by many Orthodox Christians to hold on tightly to the traditions of the past, since there have been so many who have tried to take them away. However, by clinging to the past, Orthodoxy will have a difficult time engaging in conversations with those who look to the future.

I cannot see other Christian traditions as being deviations from Orthodoxy, but rather as ways Christian faith has developed in various cultures, and in turn, how Christianity has influenced those cultures. Orthodoxy took various elements of Byzantine imperial culture, including art, architecture, and vestments, and adapted them to be ways of worshipping God and providing a structure for religious faith. It only makes sense that the Orthodox Church continue to find ways to engage culture and appropriate it toward its ends—spreading the gospel, feeding the hungry, helping the sick, championing the oppressed.

Even though I have spent nearly ten years in the Orthodox Church, I feel its hold on me starting to waver, and even though it has served as a foundation for my spiritual growth over the last decade, I am more and more content to tinker. I see the pull of the Orthodox Church on me as akin to a gravitational force. My orbit around the Orthodox Church is decaying, and the potential for me to break gravity's pull and be thrown onto a tangential path is greater and greater. However, I take comfort in that there are other forces that draw me near.

In the geometric concept of an elliptical orbit, there are two foci that guide the path of the object, each playing a vital role in the path it takes. I imagine that the Orthodox Church will always be one of my foci, but there are too many influences on my religious faith to claim that there can only be one center for this journey, and just as with an orbit, eventually I will swing closer back to the Orthodox focal point. But for now, I am content to build new creations, to tinker, to continue my spiritual journey with a strong Orthodox foundation, yet probe what it means to be part of the "one, holy, catholic, and apostolic church." And to that I say, "*Kyrie eleison.*"

DISCUSSION QUESTIONS

1. What has your faith journey been like? Are you a spiritual tinkerer? Why or why not?

2. How does your tradition respond to spiritual tinkering? What are the benefits and risks?

3. What spiritual practices (if any) does your local church borrow from other traditions? How does this impact your worship experience?

4. What cultural practices does your church uphold? Do you see benefits to maintaining these practices? What challenges would happen if they were to change?

5. What do you think about the future of Christianity in the United States in light of current trends?

NOTES

1. Alexei Krindatch's census of Orthodox Christians in the United States shows that as of 2008, 29 percent of the members of the Greek Orthodox Church Archdiocese of America and 51 percent of the Orthodox Church in

America are converts from a non-Orthodox worldview. Alexei D. Krindatch, *The Orthodox Church Today* (Berkeley, CA: Patriarch Athenagoras Orthodox Institute, 2011), http://www.hartfordinstitute.org/research/OrthChurchFull-Report.pdf, 7.

2. "The Global Religious Landscape: Religiously Unaffiliated," *The Pew Forum on Religion and Public Life,* December 18, 2012, accessed April 23, 2013, http://www.pewforum.org/global-religious-landscape-unaffiliated.aspx.

3. "'Nones' on the Rise: Executive Summary," *The Pew Forum on Religion and Public Life,* October 9, 2012, accessed April 23, 2013, http://www.pew forum.org/Unaffiliated/nones-on-the-rise.aspx.

4. Krindatch, *The Orthodox Church Today,* 58.

5. Ibid., 89.

6. Ibid., 102.

7. Ibid., 176.

8. Ibid., 90.

9. Robert Wuthnow, *After the Baby Boomers: How Twenty- and Thirty-Somethings Are Shaping the Future of American Religion* (Princeton: Princeton University Press, 2007), 13.

10. Ibid., 14.

11. Ibid.

12. Ibid., 134.

13. Ibid., 215.

14. Leonard Sweet, *Post-Modern Pilgrims: First Century Passion for the 21st Century Church* (Nashville: B&H, 2000), 72.

15. Leonard Sweet, *SoulTsunami: Sink or Swim in New Millennium Culture* (Grand Rapids: Zondervan, 1999), 210.

16. Brian McLaren, "Church Emerging: Or Why I Still Use the Word *Postmodern* but with Mixed Feelings," in Doug Pagitt and Tony Jones, eds., *An Emergent Manifesto of Hope* (Grand Rapids: Baker, 2007), 151.

17. Robert E. Webber, *Ancient-Future Faith: Rethinking Evangelicalism for a Postmodern World* (Grand Rapids: Baker, 1999), 7.

18. Alexander Schmemann, *Church, World, Mission: Reflections on Orthodoxy in the West* (Crestwood, NY: St. Vladimir's Seminary Press, 1979), 205–7.

CHAPTER 3

Living In-Beyond the Margins

A Second-Generation Immigrant Christian Experience

JAISY JOSEPH

Living in Between

Land of opportunity. This ideal has drawn millions of migrants and their children from all corners of the globe to North America, where hard work and perseverance are said to guarantee prosperity and stability. Fleeing economic, psychological, political, and social oppression, many leave the comfort of the familiar in search of freedom and hope. During the past half century, waves of immigrants have joined millions of Americans in the quest for the American dream, holding firm to the conviction that "all [people] are created equal."[1]

As a child of SyroMalabar Catholic immigrants from Kerala, India, however, I have often witnessed a different reality.[2] Whether it was observing a grocery clerk rudely dismiss my mother's questions because of her accent or having my middle school classmates ridicule my father for how he read the intercessory petitions at a school-wide Mass, I experienced the real disconnect between the ideal promise and the concrete reality. Living *in between* the Malayalee culture of my heritage and the American culture of my nationality, I never felt like I fully belonged to either.[3] I was viewed as an Indian in America by those who found "Dallas" to be an unacceptable answer to the question, "Where are you from?" I was viewed as an American in India by extended family who teased me about my inability to grasp the nuances of the Malayalam language.

Moreover, attending Roman Catholic school from Monday to Friday and SyroMalabar Catholic Church on Sundays, I never quite understood how these two expressions of the Catholic faith related to each other. The disorientation and uncertainty of living in between two cultures corresponded to the experience of living in between two expressions of the Catholic faith. I grew up confused about the purpose of establishing an Eastern Catholic community different in language, liturgy, and culture from the local parochial school I attended. I simply thought it was an Indian replica of the Roman Catholic tradition. Nevertheless, the community presented a safe haven where I no longer had to explain the particular idiosyncrasies of my heritage to curious minds. I could interact with other second-generation children who were experiencing both the positive and negative realities of our marginal status. Socialized by the ideals propagated by our culture, my friends and I strived to embody the stereotypes of "good Malayalee girls"—to excel in studies and the arts, to be respectful of elders and religious leaders, to be amiable among peers, to be well-versed spiritually and culturally, to bring honor to our parents, and to keep a pure reputation in preparation for marriage.

The myth lasted until my first year of college, when I witnessed many of my peers and role models from our community unravel under the immense pressure of living in between the expectations of both worlds. I discovered how many of us hid deep physical, emotional, psychological, and sexual wounds behind the "picture-perfect" mask we were all taught to wear in order to preserve family name and honor. Prior to college, many of us went to SyroMalabar Church not for healing, reconciliation, and authentic fellowship—not to encounter Christ—but to preserve the culture of our parents and to maintain a link to our heritage. We were unprepared for the harsh realities of college life, which brought these wounds to the surface and often inflicted new ones. Resisting the quiet despair that threatened to consume me, I questioned whether the gospel stories had any relevance to our situation. In the midst of this soul searching, I happened to take a class on liberative theologies that completely transformed my perspective.

Living in Both

I voraciously read the reflections of many Asian American and Latin theologians and was profoundly encouraged by their self-reflection. I never knew it was possible for Christian minorities to challenge patterns of injustice or for the immigrant context to reveal God. Nevertheless, I always turned the final page of the book with a sense of disappointment. Despite many parallels, none of their experiences offered solutions nor fully captured the unique experiences of a second-generation Malayalee American SyroMalabar Catholic. Yet, because tension naturally seeks resolution, theologians such as Jung Young Lee inspired me to reimagine the theological and existential value of being a culturally hyphenated Eastern Catholic.

Lee constructs a valuable interpretation of marginality that highlights the experience of migrants and their children as *in-between* and *in-both* the North American culture and the heritage culture. To be in between multiple centers is to emphasize the experience of double negation. For example, when I felt that I was Indian in America and American in India, it was as though I belonged fully to neither sphere. Such marginal experiences contribute to an existential experience of nonbeing, an "existential *nothingness* caused by the perspective of two (or more) dominant worlds." This existential nothingness leads to an experience of dehumanization.[4] Nevertheless, the self-negating experience of being in-between is counterbalanced and complemented by the self-affirming experience of being in both worlds. While not replacing the negative experiences of being in-between, to be in-both is to affirm the good that emerges from the heritage of one's roots *and* the culture of one's residence. Moreover, this genuine appreciation of one's roots fosters an appreciation for the origins of others.[5]

Maintaining the negative experiences of being in-between and the positive experiences of being in-both may appear contradictory. Yet, Lee argues, both aspects constitute one reality for migrants and their children. Marginality, therefore, is to exist at the very "margin that connects both worlds."[6] At the same time, by living immanently in both, it enables the possibility of transcending both worlds. Thus, to be simultaneously in-between and in-both is to be *in-beyond*.[7] Further defining the reality of being *in-beyond*, Lee claims that

> *to transcend or to live in-beyond does not mean to be free of the two different worlds in which persons exist, but to live in both of them without being bound by either of them.* The new marginal person is a liberated person, a person who is truly free, because each is a whole person and able to be fully present in the world. Because the new marginal person is whole, he or she reconciles two opposing worlds unto the self. The new marginal person is a reconciler and a wounded healer to the two-category system.[8]

While encouraged by how Lee provided language to describe my own context as a child of immigrants, I was more inspired by how he related the marginal experience to the life of Jesus Christ. Lee argues that the human inclination to seek the center as the position of power has often led Christians to focus more on Christ's lordship than his servanthood.[9] The Philippian hymn speaks of a divine marginalization, however, when it describes how the Son "did not regard equality with God something to be exploited, but emptied himself, taking the form of a slave" (Philippians 2:6-7).

In the Incarnation, God became empty for the sake of serving humanity.[10] Though not empty in essence, the Son denied himself to such an extent that he "humbled himself and became obedient to the point of death—even death on a cross" (Philippians 2:8). Slaves, by definition, do not belong to the dominant group. Although possessing the nature of God, the Son was incarnated in the form of a slave "to become the precise margin of marginality."[11] Placed in between two worlds, Jesus experienced total negation in order to totally affirm himself in both worlds. His total self-emptying occurred simultaneously with his total self-fulfillment. Because as servant he was obedient even unto death, God "also highly exalted" him and gave him "the name that is above every name" (Philippians 2:9). Thus, the "humiliation of Christ simultaneously accompanies his exultation."[12]

While this hymn from Philippians tells the story of marginalization from the divine perspective, the Gospels narrate Jesus' life of marginality from the human perspective. Conceived within the womb of an unwed mother, born among animals in a stable, and forced to flee to Egypt in response to Herod's persecution, Jesus began his life on the margins. Marginality continued to characterize his public ministry. He lived as a homeless man and associated himself with the poor and the oppressed, the sick and the afflicted. Behind the inspiring teachings and miraculous healings stood a humble man who chose this life in order to serve. Jesus lived "in the world, but not of it. He negated the world as a beggar, but affirmed it as a servant."[13] Living simultaneously in-between and in-both, Jesus modeled what it means to truly live in-beyond. Jesus Christ was "the new marginal person *par excellence*."[14] To be a Christian disciple is to imitate Christ by also being in the world but not of the world—to simultaneously totally affirm and totally negate this world.[15]

Living In-Beyond

After reading Lee's insights regarding the theological significance of the marginal experience, I saw Christ with new eyes. For the first time, I no longer looked toward others' marginal experiences for solutions, but saw them as guideposts that led me in a new way to Christ, who experienced the depth of marginality throughout his life. Christ is the one who can ultimately show the way through despair. Only by embracing the realities of living in between and in both worlds will my community have a glimpse of the Christian freedom promised by the in-beyond. Our marginal status is not an obstacle to an abundant life, (John 10:10) but a means of identifying with Christ, who came so that we may imitate him who is "the way, and the truth, and the [abundant] life" (John 14:6).

Encouraged by Lee's insights and my own reflections on them, I wanted to understand the specific forces that shaped the positive and negative aspects of my community's context in North America. With a deeper understanding of how our situation came to be, I hoped to work with others in changing the direction of our generation from quiet despair to the new life promised at our baptism. Numerous conversations with our bishop and youth leaders from various communities throughout the United States revealed that the apathy of the second generation was not based on the innate indifference presumed by the immigrant generation. Rather, this apparent apathy was actually caused by a sense of rootlessness and disconnect with our heritage and a profound confusion regarding the relevance of the SyroMalabar Catholic faith in our search for meaning and truth in a new context.

My research also led me to discover a definition formulated by prominent SyroMalabar historian Dr. Placid Podipara, CMI. He describes a community of Christians who trace their origins to the evangelization of the apostle Thomas, as *Christian in faith, Syrian in worship, and Indian in culture.* Fascinated by how my ancestors were formed by this ancient expression of Christianity, I wrote my honors thesis on this topic and titled it "The Struggle for Identity among SyroMalabar Catholics." My ancestors not only lived their faith in the midst of a Hindu-dominated context and enriched their tradition with Syriac liturgy, spirituality, and theology, but they also resisted the latinizations of European colonizers.

The tensions of contemporary migrations, therefore, are but the latest chapter in a nearly two-thousand-year struggle to pass the Christian tradition from generation to generation. After Bishop Jacob Angadiath and several priests shared their enthusiasm for this thesis during their homilies, numerous conversations erupted throughout the diocese. These conversations began to connect many young people and priests who desired more for our community. We often gathered together to pray about how we could make our faith communities relevant to both generations as a place of healing, reconciliation, and authentic fellowship—a place of encounter with Christ.

A Vision for the Future

While we dreamed and prayed together, a vision for the future and well-being of our community began to unfold organically after 2008. First, we recognized the immense riches available through our Western education. As many resources regarding SyroMalabar Catholic history, liturgy, theology, and spirituality are reserved in Kerala for seminarians, many of the faithful there have little access to this information. However, these books are readily available in the libraries of major Western universities. In addition, many of our young people have the opportunity to explore these topics as research projects for their history and theology courses. This realization led to the birth of *Syro Study,* an annual gathering of young, committed scholars who wish to explore any aspect of interest that can illumine our context in North America. With the support of Dr. Peter Casarella from the Center for World Catholicism and Intercultural Theology at DePaul University, we explored themes related to the Second Vatican Council and the significance of the communion of churches. Future topics include the liturgy, the theology of St. Ephraim, and the global diaspora of Thomas Christians. This young initiative provides a necessary base within the community to strengthen our intellectual understanding of the spiritual gift we have received so that we may become a gift to others by sharing this heritage.

Second, we prayed for young people called from within our generation to serve our community through the unique awareness of what it means to be in-between and in-both worlds. Not only to our astonishment, but also to the surprise of many in Kerala who doubted the flourishing of a SyroMalabar Catholic diocese outside of India, several young people have discerned a call to leave potential careers in medicine and business to enter the seminary and pursue academic theology. Experiencing the cry of our generation, many have felt called to serve the church in ways that witness to its deep relevance beyond cultural preservation.

Finally, this early vision sought to raise a consciousness within our generation by providing a space where questions of life and faith could be honestly explored from the perspective of the second generation. In 2009, we held the first Diocesan Youth Leaders Gathering (DYLG) that summoned young leaders from youth groups across the nation to the cathedral in Chicago and provided seminars on faith and the church, encouraged group discussions and action-planning sessions, and offered ample opportunities for personal prayer, the sacrament of reconciliation, and communal prayer before the blessed sacrament. We are grateful for the fruits of this first gathering, which encouraged many to return to their regions and lead conferences in the Northeast, South, West, Mid-Atlantic, and Southeast. Whereas parishes used to emphasize the cultural formation of their youth, these conferences encouraged a holistic faith formation.

In October 2011, Cardinal Mar George Alencherry, the head and father of the SyroMalabar Catholic Church, appointed thirteen young people as the first national coordinators of the Diocesan Youth Apostolate. The charter defines this apostolate as "a communion of youth groups and ministries [that unite] all young people of the Diocese in response to the gospel message of Jesus Christ by encouraging the formation of a deep interior life that overflows into genuine service to the Church and to the world." Comprised of young women and men from various parts of the United States and with varying levels of experience with the SyroMalabar tradition, this group not only focuses on the hopes and struggles of the young people, but also serves as a bridge between the second generation, the immigrant generation, and the church hierarchy.

A Call to Action

Reflecting on the past years in light of God's providence, the zeal of the young people has surprised the immigrant generation and the hierarchy. With their trust and support, we are beginning to understand the church less as a bastion of cultural preservation and more as an unique expression and witness of the Catholic faith. Yet we also have much to accomplish if we are to enable our faith community to become a place of healing, reconciliation, and authentic fellowship—a place of encounter with Christ.

First, to experience authentically the liberation of living in-beyond, we must enable ourselves to emerge from behind the picture-perfect masks. We must strive for the creation of safe spaces where young people can come as they are, with all of their imperfections and without the fear of tarnishing family honor, to personally experience the hope of the Christian message that has been passed down from our ancestors for nearly two millennia. The maintenance of such masks encourages duplicity, which becomes an obstacle to self-discovery. If the church provides an environment that inspires their removal, then it is possible for more young people to experience the new life described by the gospel. This new life promises the freedom to be not only as we are but to become what we are called to be through Christian discipleship.

Second, because the church community often provides the only intergenerational space outside of the home, this space becomes an opportunity to build understanding between parents and their children. Both generations are chained by particular struggles that are not easily translatable. The trauma of immigration, including the discrimination often experienced in transit and within the new situation of settlement, often remains unprocessed and unarticulated by many of the first generation as they try to justify their losses through the accumulation of wealth and the achievements of their children. Meanwhile, torn between their Malayalee up-bringing and their American socialization, the second generation often feels misunderstood by their parents, who, because they experienced a homogenized culture back home, are often insensitive to the necessary struggle for self-discovery within their children.

There is a need for the pastoral care of those who are wounded within the community. However, we must also engage in acts of justice and service beyond the walls of our church. Particularly as the daughters and sons of immigrants, we cannot remain aloof as our sisters and brothers die along the US-Mexico border for the same rights that we so gratuitously enjoy. We must offer the solidarity and hospitality that our parents rarely experienced when they first arrived here. United by similar experiences of living in between and in both worlds, we must strive to live in-beyond our own sufferings and realize how our experiences encourage a profound empathy and love for others. Indeed, every time we offer the Holy Qurbana (liturgy) "for all those who suffer and are in distress, the poor and the oppressed, the sick and the afflicted,"[16] may we hear a call to action. This call should convince us that the healing, reconciliation, and authentic fellowship that we strive for within our community must overflow and generate hope among others. By taking advantage of such opportunities to practice self and communal transcendence within this "land of opportunity," may we continually imitate Jesus Christ as we strive for the in-beyond.

DISCUSSION QUESTIONS

1. Do you live in in-between and in-both worlds, as the author describes? If not, whom do you know who does?

2. What are the theological books or resources that have transformed your perspective as a Christian?

3. What kind of space does your church need to create so that people can emerge from behind their masks and seek to live life in Christ?

4. What are/were the struggles of your parents' generation? How do they relate to the struggles of your generation?

5. What is the church's role with regard to immigration? What is our role as individual Christians?

NOTES

1. US Declaration of Independence, accessed April 19, 2013, http://www.archives.gov/exhibits/charters/declaration_transcript.html.

2. The SyroMalabar Church is one of twenty-two Eastern Catholic Churches in full communion with the Roman Catholic Church.

3. Malayalee is an adjective that describes those who come from Kerala, a state on the southwest coast of India.

4. Jung Young Lee, *Marginality: The Key to Multicultural Theology* (Minneapolis: Fortress Press, 1995), 45.

5. Ibid., 50.

6. Ibid., 60.

7. Ibid.

8. Ibid., 63; italics in original.

9. Ibid., 78.

10. Ibid., 82.

11. Ibid.

12. Ibid., 83.

13. Ibid., 89.

14. Ibid., 72.

15. Ibid.

16. This is a common prayer of petition during the SyroMalabar liturgy.

CHAPTER 4

Global Christianities

New Immigrant Church Growth and the Protestant Mainline

JENNIFER T. LANCASTER

Global Christianities

Throughout US history, waves of immigration have brought significant changes to the religious landscape. In the decades since Congress passed the 1965 Immigration and Nationalities Act, such changes have included not only the arrival of the spectrum of the world's religions, but a range of global *Christianities* as well. As Christians from Africa, Asia, Latin America, and South America have come to call the United States home, they have brought with them forms and practices of Christianity influenced by their own cultures, traditions, and social norms.

In some cases, immigrant Christians are coming from places with deep ties to the international missionary work of churches in the United States, namely, Protestant churches. This reality is raising critical questions about the future. How are these denominations responding to current immigration trends in the United States? What is the relationship between immigrant churches and these denominations? How is God calling all of us to live into this new reality together?

Over the past few years, I have worked closely with a Presbyterian congregation of Oromo Ethiopian immigrants in Lancaster, Pennsylvania. In relationship with them, I have experienced the vital role that immigrant congregations can play in the revitalization of Protestant churches. I believe their story can shed some light on how we might begin to think about the challenges and opportunities before us as denominations seek to engage in new ways with global Christian communities in the United States.

Oromo Evangelical Church

The US Immigration Act of 1990 established the diversity visa, a government-sponsored program established "to stimulate 'new seed' immigration from parts of the world that are underrepresented in the US."[1] Within a decade, nearly fifty thousand immigrants had arrived in the United States with newly issued green cards through this program—almost half of whom were immigrants from Africa, including nearly four thousand from Ethiopia. The Oromo people, who make up the largest ethnic group in Ethiopia, received the majority of these Ethiopian visas.[2] As a result, the 1990s saw the formation and growth of several Oromo-speaking congregations in the United States.[3]

In 1994 several Oromo immigrants living in north Philadelphia began a small prayer group. As interest grew, the group began meeting at Summit Presbyterian Church on Greene Street in West Mt. Airy, and within two years, forty-one Oromo Ethiopians were attending Sunday services. Eventually the Philadelphia Oromo fellowship moved to a suburban location to accommodate worshippers driving from points as far west as Lancaster and Harrisburg. During this transition, the fellowship was nested with another Presbyterian church, the Central Presbyterian Church in Downingtown.

In 2006 the congregation in Downingtown decided to become two separate congregations, one back in Philadelphia and one even farther west in Lancaster County. The weekly trip from Lancaster to Downingtown, and the rising cost of gasoline, had taken its toll on the growing Lancaster community. Donegal Presbytery arranged for the growing Oromo congregation to nest—or share building space and community life—with a struggling English-speaking church in Lancaster, Bethany Presbyterian Church—a common kind of pairing. Today the Oromo Evangelical Church in Lancaster is the only Oromo congregation within the Presbyterian Church (USA).

Over the past one hundred years, the conflict-ridden social, political, and cultural context of the Oromo people in Ethiopia provided fertile ground for Christianity to take root and flourish. Beginning in the early twentieth century with Presbyterian and Lutheran mission efforts, missionaries saw themselves as bearers of both the Christian gospel and modernity. With the Bible in one hand and medical technologies in the other, efforts to grow the church in Ethiopia were very successful. Protestant Christianity continues to flourish throughout Oromia to this day.

Most Oromo Christian immigrants to the United States seek to maintain their Christian identity, oftentimes in relationship to these missionary "sending bodies" in the United States. At the same time, they seek to sustain religious beliefs and practices built around their ethnic Oromo identity. The Oromo Evangelical Church in Lancaster is an example of a racial ethnic minority group in the PC(USA) that is continuing the traditions of its culture while creating a new relationship with an established Christian institution in the United States.

Immigrant Churches and Mainline Growth

In recent years, the desire for church membership to reflect more fully the rapidly changing demographics of US society, combined with steady membership decline, has led several Mainline Protestant denominations to develop formal strategies for increasing racial ethnic diversity. In 1996, for example, the General Assembly of the PC(USA) approved the "Racial Ethnic Immigrant Evangelism Church Growth Strategy" as a tool for the denomination to actively create new immigrant church fellowships and, in turn, to begin to increase the percentage of racial and ethnic minorities in the denomination.

At that time, only 4.7 percent of the church's membership was reported as nonwhite. The Growth Strategy noted that while most of the PC(USA) represents an "Anglo, suburban, and middle-class denomination," this does not reflect the wider demographic trends taking shape in society.[4] The document outlined a growth strategy aiming for racial ethnic diversity within the denomination to reach 20 percent by 2010. However, as the years passed, the actual numbers fell well below those goals. By 2005 the rate had increased to 8.1 percent and by 2010 to only 9.1 percent.[5]

During the 2010 meeting of the PC(USA) General Assembly, a task force was commissioned to study how and why the denomination fell short of the 1998 goals. Named the Task Force on Racial Ethnic and New Immigrant Church Growth, this group spent two years conducting polls and interviews in an attempt to discern the shortcomings. Further, the task force was charged with making new recommendations for attaining future growth in racial ethnic diversity. In July 2012 the task force submitted its final report, "Growing a Diverse Church: A Call for Unity and Reconciliation," to the General Assembly, identifying many challenges but offering little in terms of new strategies for the future.

The experience of the Oromo Evangelical Church (OEC) of Philadelphia illustrates the shortcomings of the growth strategy and the challenges all denominations face as they build strategies to support new immigrant church growth. In 1999 the OEC submitted a New Church Development Probe to the General Assembly of the PC(USA), initiating the lengthy process of becoming a member congregation within the Presbytery of Philadelphia. The initial grant covered operating and program expenses as well as funds for pastoral leadership training.

In February 2004 the General Assembly received an additional grant proposal from OEC, indicating that the church sought to enter the New Church Development (NCD) phase with the hopes of becoming a full PC(USA) congregation in the future. The General Assembly awarded the congregation a declining grant that included funding provided by all three levels of Presbyterian governance, with the General Assembly contributing the highest amount, followed by the Synod of the Trinity, and the Donegal Presbytery. The grant money would carry the Oromo New Church Development to the end of 2011, at which time the church could proceed toward the status of a chartered congregation.[6]

The grant anticipated financial independence of the Oromo NCD by 2011, which was predicated on significant growth in membership. When the fellowship began keeping membership records in 1997, there were only twenty members. By the time of the second grant application in 2004, the fellowship had increased to eighty members. According to the terms of the grant, the church was expected to exceed a hundred members by 2007 and 137 by the end of 2010. As of October 2012 Oromo Evangelical Church membership stood at ninety-one, far below the goal set forth in the grant, and the expected financial sustainability never came to fruition. As a result, Oromo Evangelical Church had to terminate its NCD status and transition back into a church fellowship.

In hindsight it is clear that the budget contained assumptions and expectations about financial growth within the community that were unrealistic and perhaps culturally insensitive. Most members were working low-income jobs and sending remittances to the homeland, thus limiting the available capital for sustaining the congregation. What was lacking in the grant was a full awareness of the challenging realities of the congregants at OEC and a strategic plan that took these realities into account.

Changing Church Structures

As the landscape of American Christianity continues to change, the structures of denominations in the United States, including the mainline Protestant churches, must also change in order to embrace the realities faced by immigrant churches such as the

Oromo Evangelical Church. While denominational bodies look for ways to empower immigrant congregations to become self-sufficient, they need to see economic viability as only one part of the equation. As in the OEC case, it might be ineffective and costly for any denomination to rely solely on statistical growth projections and budgetary increases as indicators for success. Rather, new models of sustainability are required to truly impact the flourishing of immigrant churches.

For example, welcoming and shepherding new immigrant communities and fostering internal leadership are other ways denominational bodies can begin to empower congregants in these churches. In some instances, this might include creating nested immigrant congregations within an existing congregation, or it might simply involve allowing an immigrant fellowship access to church space for worship. As I was concluding my fieldwork with OEC, discussions were happening that would involve the creation of a multicultural ministry in the building of Bethany Presbyterian Church. In the proposed ministry, one church building would be home to four distinct congregations: the immigrant Oromo group, the already established Bethany group (primarily older, white congregants), a Latino congregation, and a newly formed missional outreach church plant. This particular project was being overseen by local church leadership (the local presbytery) with a goal of raising up leaders within each group to sustain that congregation.

Reverend Ray Meute, a local PC(USA) pastor in Pennsylvania, supports this sentiment: "Our denomination used to have an involved, expensive process for developing new congregations, but today, we are finding we can't do it that way anymore. . . . There has been a lot of money allocated, but now we need to find other ways of supporting them." He continued by arguing that "the denomination's long-standing model isn't working; it isn't financially sustainable."[7] If the denomination's latest goal—to establish 1001 new worship communities across the country by 2022—is to be achieved, traditional models of church and church organization must be reconsidered.

In an age of economic instability and membership decline, how can churches in the United States partner with immigrant fellowships to become self-supporting and self-sufficient? As church structures at all levels are experiencing budgetary cutbacks, they are no longer able to maintain former levels of financial support. At the same time, it is clear that the current top-down model does not necessarily produce viable immigrant congregations, nor does it cultivate overall denomination growth. While the "PC(USA)'s membership is becoming ethnically broader [through new church developments], it's not growing overall."[8] Reasons for this stagnation are varied, but generally, congregants leave to attend different churches, older members die, and birthrates among members are low. This trend is not isolated to the Presbyterian Church (USA). Across denominational lines, growth is in many ways inhibited. In turn, to effectively encourage growth, definitions of sustainability will need to become more holistic, not simply focused on creating new immigrant congregations. New kinds of partnerships must be forged between established congregations and immigrant congregations, offering ongoing accompaniment and mutual support to all involved.

Over the last ten years, the PC(USA) has chartered seventeen new congregations, along with a number of so-called "expensive failures." Will the Oromo Evangelical Church be one of those failures? As I interact with this congregation on a weekly basis, it is difficult to consider this devout and faithful community as a failure of any sort. Although they currently lack ordained pastoral leadership, the group thrives on the biblical promises of faith and endurance. So, while OEC does not meet the standards for a chartered congregation within the PC(USA) at this time, there are signs that the church will secure both church leadership and a sustainable future.

The OEC, like many other immigrant congregations, is presenting a pressing challenge to American Christianity to redefine what it means to be a church today. Many factors—whether social, cultural, racial, or theological—contribute to the challenges of immigrant congregational growth and sustainability, and current structures provide little flexibility. Denominations must recognize how the arrival of global Christianities in this country will inherently alter time-honored, traditional, and homogenous characterizations of *what it means to be Christian, what it means to be the church*. As a result, and in order to remain effective, denominations must create new ways of welcoming, nurturing, and growing with immigrant congregations, and receiving their gifts in turn. This is the challenge and the opportunity before us all.

DISCUSSION QUESTIONS

1. What are your ethnic roots?

2. Does your denomination seek to increase its racial ethnic diversity through immigrant congregations? If so, what structures and strategies are in place to foster this growth?

3. Oromo Evangelical Church congregants worship in the Oromo language and sing songs that are native to their homeland. What cultural traditions does your church maintain?

4. Congregants at Oromo Evangelical Church are currently worshipping each Sunday with no ordained pastor leading the church. How important is lay leadership in your congregation? How might leadership be built up from within congregations?

5. Rather than relying on a top-down financial structure for new immigrant congregations, what other kinds of creative strategies might lead to their financial sustainability?

NOTES

1. "The Diversity Visa System: A Fact Sheet," *Immigration Policy Center*, April 4, 2011, accessed April 23, 2013, http://www.immigrationpolicy.org/just-facts/diversity-visa-system-fact-sheet.

2. Ibid.

3. Throughout the 1990s, Oromo-speaking congregations were forming in Washington, DC and Minneapolis, along with smaller prayer groups in Atlanta, Portland, Seattle, and Dallas.

4. "Racial Ethnic Immigrant Evangelism Church Growth Strategy," *Presbyterian Church (USA)*, April 12, 2006, accessed April 23, 2013, http://www.pcusa.org/resource/racial-ethnic-and-immigrant-church-growth-strategy/.

5. Jason P. Reagan, "Racial-Ethnic Members Show Percentage Upswing as PC(USA) Numbers Falter," *The Layman*, July 7, 2011, accessed April 23, 2013, http://www.layman.org/Files/Layman%20-%20July%20201123bf.pdf.

6. "General Assembly Mission Program Grant: New Congregation Grant Application" Office of Mission Program Grants, *Presbyterian Church (USA)*, February 29, 2004.

7. Telephone interview, Reverend Ray Meute, February 14, 2012.

8. Reagan, "Racial-Ethnic Members Show Percentage Upswing."

CHAPTER 5

The Scandal of Main Street Steeples

Christian Unity for Everyday Life

PAUL DAVID BROWN

Scandalous Division

It was a beautiful, late summer morning, and I was driving a car full of groomsmen to a friend's wedding ceremony. As we wound through the tranquil countryside of upstate New York on the way to the church, the conversation turned to religion. Sitting next to me in the passenger seat, the best man asked about my studies in divinity school, and we started talking about some of the differences between Christian denominations. About halfway through our discussion, we followed Route 21 into the tiny village of Palmyra.

There, at the intersection of Main and Canandaigua Streets, our eyes could not help but drift up to notice four soaring church steeples that pierced the sky. On each corner of the intersection stood a different church—Baptist, Methodist, Presbyterian, and Episcopal. The best man, who attended a suburban nondenominational congregation, remarked how he had never really thought about Christian division until he saw it dramatically displayed on that street corner. As it turns out, another young man, Joseph

Smith, had been bothered by that very same intersection more than a hundred years earlier. Born and raised in Palmyra, Smith's frustration with the competing churches in town contributed to his overall disillusionment with traditional Christianity. In the end, the scandal of Christian division—brought to life on a remote corner in New York—gave birth to even more division and the new religious movement of Mormonism.

In today's world, which seems more polarized than ever, the church's disunity is a scandalous contradiction of the Good News at the heart of the Christian faith: that Jesus Christ has reconciled us to God and to each other. Faced with growing numbers of nonreligious persons and questions about the future of organized religion, Christians living in the United States today must begin to imagine new ways of overcoming our divisions.

Why Unity Is Important for Christians

The scandal of Main Street steeples in cities and towns such as Palmyra across the United States presents a basic challenge to the church: Why should anyone take our message seriously if we refuse to practice what we preach? Shortly before his death on the cross, Jesus prayed "on behalf of those who will believe in me through their [the disciples'] word, that they may all be one . . . that the world may believe that you [Father] have sent me" (John 17:20-21). The apostle Paul described the church as the body of Christ—the continuation of Jesus' ministry in the world—"for in the one Spirit we were all baptized into one body" (1 Corinthians 12:13). Just as Jesus came to reconcile us to God through his life, death, and resurrection, now he has "entrust[ed] the message of reconciliation to us" (2 Corinthians 5:19). But how can Christians preach with integrity about Jesus' reconciling work on the cross while refusing to be reconciled to each other? By allowing pride to take priority over love, the church has compromised its witness. As Paul wrote to the Christians in the ancient city of Corinth, "If I have all faith, so as to remove mountains, but do not have love, I am nothing" (1 Corinthians 13:2).

With all the divisions in the church, some have concluded that Christian unity is an impossible goal. The best anyone can hope for, they say, is a kind of unity in certain ideas. I would argue, though, that if we abandon the quest for Christian unity, we not only perpetuate the scandal of Main Street steeples, but we risk living in continual disobedience to the prayer of our Lord Jesus and the words of Scripture. Instead of giving up, as Christians we must humble ourselves and trust in the power of God's Holy Spirit to "accomplish abundantly far more than all we can ask or imagine" (Ephesians 3:20). One of the great champions of Christian unity in the twentieth century, Lesslie Newbigin, once said that "for too long, the churches have argued over what they are—surely it is time for us to meet one another in penitent acknowledgment of our common failure to be what we ought to be."[1] The Bible teaches that the Spirit is at work in us as individuals, leading us on the journey of salvation toward wholehearted love of God and others. In the same way, the Spirit is nudging the church, inviting us to become a community of reconciliation and love that embodies God's intentions for the whole world. If we remain content with our divisions, then yes, a reconciled church will forever be impossible. But what if, instead, we listened to the words of Jesus' prayer? What if we responded to the open invitation of the Spirit? What would a united church look like today?

A Movement for Christian Unity

Beginning in the late 1800s, many Christians began to imagine together what Christian unity might actually look like in everyday life. On the other side of the world from the sleepy town of Palmyra, missionaries from different churches started asking themselves this question: Why should the old divisions of European and American Christians be imposed on new churches in other parts of the world? Why replicate the scandal of Main Street steeples? Wouldn't missionaries be stronger evangelists if they were working together? Driven by questions like these, Protestant missionaries from across the globe gathered in Scotland for a conference in 1910.[2] There the chairman joined the church's mission with the quest for Christian unity, calling for "the evangelism of the world in this generation" under the motto of Jesus' prayer "that they may all be one" (John 17:20).

Springing from this conference, a remarkable thing happened. Christians of various backgrounds and denominations from all over the world started to think about new possibilities for Christian unity, the beginnings of what would come to be called the modern "ecumenical movement." The more they talked, the more they realized that many of the things they had always believed about each other simply were not true or not properly understood. As the ecumenical movement picked up steam, the World Council of Churches, established in 1937, became the main global forum for dialogue, advocacy, and education among Christians. In the United States, the National Council of the Churches of Christ in the USA was formed in 1950.

Among Protestants around the world, this dialogue quickly led to significant steps on the road to unity. In some cases, two or more churches decided to shed their denominational labels and merge, most notably among Protestants in Canada (1925), Thailand (1934), South India (1947), the Philippines (1948), the United States (1957), Zambia (1965), North India (1970), and Australia (1977). In the early 1960s, a substantial movement among several Protestant churches in the United States—the Consultation on Church Union (COCU)—came together to explore the possibility of union. While significant consensus was reached, progress toward merger began to break down over differences in church structures along with the lingering threat of institutional racism. Additionally, some worried that the bureaucracy of a large united Protestant denomination could drag down the mission of local churches.

After a proposal for merger was overwhelmingly rejected in 1970, talks among Protestants in the United States began to move toward "full communion," where churches recognize each other's ministers and seek to collaborate in mission. Several churches in the United States have reached full communion, but the fruits of these agreements have been slow to ripen, at least in the eyes of people in the pews. Today some Christians talk about the churches entering an "ecumenical winter," where the momentum building toward unity has slowed dramatically.

Challenges to Christian Unity

From its very beginnings, many have dismissed the quest for Christian unity as sitting around and singing "Kumbaya," or as a wishy-washy resignation to the lowest common denominator. In the fundamentalist congregations of my childhood in the 1980s and '90s, the ecumenical movement was denounced as a dangerous compromise of the truth. We believed the best way to protect unity in the church was to separate from anyone who disagreed with our pastor's particular understanding of Christian teachings. Still, from time to time, guest preachers or new members would offer a competing interpretation of the Bible. With both sides pointing to the same passages of Scripture with equal passion and conviction, I remember asking, "How do I know who is right?" The answer I often received was as unconvincing to me as it must have been to Joseph Smith years ago: "Because I said so."

While fundamentalism survives in certain Christian circles today, the past half century has witnessed the rise of new, far-reaching changes in American religion. Turned off by the dogmatism of fundamentalism, many American Christians increasingly understand their faith in an intensely personal way, unbound by any holy book, leader, denomination, or creed. In coffee shops and on college campuses, a growing religiously unaffiliated population that identifies as "spiritual but not religious" is content to pick and choose from a variety of religious traditions and experiences. This way of thinking resists labels and ideas of absolute truth and creates meaning through an ever-expanding set of personal preferences and experiences.

The effect of this shift in thinking has had a profound impact on American churches. Thousands of independent "nondenominational" congregations that appeal to spiritual seekers from across the religious spectrum have sprung up in every town across the country. In place of the pews and hymnals found in traditional churches, nondenominational Christians enjoy stadium seating from which they praise God in time with Christian rock music. Still, in spite of their reaction against denominationalism, these congregations have too often avoided the hard work of Christian unity, preferring a postmodern vision of the church as a decentralized network of individuals and communities. Meanwhile, the historic "mainline" Protestant denominations that once explored the possibility of union have suffered a hemorrhaging of members that only continues to accelerate.

While many American Christians now attend nondenominational churches, millions more no longer go to church or identify with any particular religion at all. Most of these individuals still believe in God but have abandoned religious affiliation in favor of a more personal spirituality. In 2012 it was reported that the number of nonreligious Americans increased 5 percent in five years to one-fifth of the country's population. Among my generation, known as "millennials" (born after 1980), the percentage increases to one-third, signaling rough times ahead for all religious groups in America.[3]

Given the many challenges facing the churches in the coming years, what are we to make of those Main Street steeples in Palmyra? Were the fundamentalists right? Should we abandon the search for unity with other Christians in favor of defending our unique "brand"? Does the rise of nondenominational churches signal a new age of postdenominational unity—or of even greater division at the congregational level? And what will become of the old Protestant congregations on that Palmyra street corner? Are they destined to one day close their doors, with their steeples serving only as a memorial to a day gone by, to a Christianity undone by its own divisions?

Imagining a Way Forward

After abandoning fundamentalism in college, I nearly gave up on the church until I started visiting a nearby United Methodist congregation. There I found a home in a tradition that values unity in diversity. John Wesley, who started Methodism as a renewal movement in the Church of England in the 1700s, reached out to other Christians in his own day, saying, "If we cannot as yet think alike in all things, at least we may love alike."[4] Like a single voice in a choir or a thread in a tapestry, the United Methodists I met were proud of their church's unique gifts but understood themselves as "one small part" of a greater whole.[5] In the fertile ground of contemporary American soil, I believe there are many other Christians who are hungry for this third way between the closed-minded rigidity of fundamentalism and the kind of vague spirituality that finds "ancient religions dull but themselves uniquely fascinating."[6]

Along with the many challenges facing churches today, exciting opportunities for common ground are opening up as the country grows more diverse and open-minded. In the past, religion was avoided in polite conversation or confined to professional theologians in an ivory tower. Today most of our personally held religious views are publically displayed on Facebook. Discussions about religious differences come up at home, at work, at school, and online. In my own experience, I have been changed by the profound spiritual testimony of my Pentecostal neighbor; I am continually humbled by the devotion of my Catholic friends who attend daily Mass; and by learning from my Greek Orthodox professor, I have a come to a deeper awareness of the beauty of God. In our day-to-day interactions with other Christians, many people are discovering a newfound sense of appreciation for the unique gifts that we have to share with each other. And beneath the surface of the growing nondenominational, new monastic, and emerging church movements, there are thousands of young Christians who are ready to see the church move beyond the denominational bickering and institutional posturing that have paralyzed its witness in the past.

American Christians are also rediscovering the connection between Christian unity and mission. As the country becomes less religious and at the same time increasingly multireligious, Christians of all backgrounds have found that what we share through our faith in Jesus Christ is much bigger than what we allow to divide us. New ecumenical possibilities are beginning to emerge. For example, through the "Circle of Protection," groups that were once distant, such as the National Council of Churches, the National Association of Evangelicals, and the US Conference of Catholic Bishops, have recently joined together with other Christian leaders to advocate for protections for the poor, whom Jesus called "the least of these" (Matthew 25:40).[7] On a more local level, in the town of Gastonia, North Carolina, where I first served as a United Methodist pastor, my congregation joined with evangelical and historically black churches to distribute food and repair homes for underprivileged families in our neighborhood. As we stand side by side, it becomes increasingly clear that we can have a greater impact on the community when we are willing to work together.

Is it possible that such partnerships—as signs of an expanded Christian table and a shared commitment to be in service to the gospel—might one day lead to reconciliation on a larger scale? While it's important to remember that any progress toward unity requires patience and humility, we should also keep in mind Jesus' words to his disciples, that "what is impossible for mortals is possible for God" (Luke 18:27). As people who have been given the incredible task of extending God's mission of reconciliation to the ends of the earth, I think we can afford to dream big! What would it take to reconcile the scandalous divisions of Main Streets across America in our own time? While there is no single way forward for the churches, what are some concrete ways that Christians can join together in everyday life that celebrate the diversity of our different traditions?

Key Shifts for a New Paradigm

First, unity in diversity requires a shift in *self-identity*. Not far from my former church in Gastonia there is a small liberal arts Catholic college founded by Benedictine monks. The brothers can be seen moving quietly around campus today and meeting regularly in the abbey church for prayers. While remaining undeniably united in their faith with Catholics in other religious orders, the Benedictines have been able to maintain their own distinctive emphases and practices.

What if Protestant Christians began thinking about unity in the same way? What if, instead of understanding denominations as ends in themselves, all Protestants saw themselves as being part of distinctive "orders" united by a common faith but free to celebrate the diversity of gifts that each tradition brings to the larger church? While paying lip service to unity, most Protestant denominations and congregations continue to operate in isolation, defined more by their distinctiveness than by what they share. How might a fresh expression of a common faith move beyond these denominational divisions and open up new ways of being undeniably united? Could this shift in self-identity one day allow Protestants to participate in a more fruitful dialogue with their Catholic and Orthodox sisters and brothers?

Second, unity in diversity requires a shift in *direction*. In contrast to the top-down mergers and joint statements brokered by official denominational representatives in the twentieth century, the new work of Christian unity must begin at the local level. Like the theologically and racially diverse group of churches that worked together in my community, Christians in towns and cities around the country are already experiencing the presence of God in each other and can no longer be the same. By holding together unity and mission at the local level, more and more American churches are beginning to move past old stereotypes and divisions.

As these relationships continue to develop, what if mainline Protestants could let go of their former positions of privilege in society and recover a missional identity as smaller, more vibrant denominations? At the same time, what if evangelicals and non-denominational Protestants could adopt a broader vision of unity that reaches beyond the individual or congregational level and actively engages more fully with Catholic, Orthodox, and other Protestant churches in their communities?

Across the United States, ordinary Christians of all denominations are coming to see themselves as one part of a greater whole that is grounded in a common mission. I believe that far from being stuck in the dead of an ecumenical winter, a fresh spring breeze is beginning to blow. God's Spirit is nudging Christians everywhere, inviting us to embrace a shared unity in the midst of our diversity. Together a new generation of Christians can offer a compelling third way that avoids the twin pitfalls of narrow fundamentalism and disconnected spirituality. Together we can speak with one voice of God's love for all in a society that is increasingly polarized between people of different faiths and people of no faith at all. Together we can pray with Jesus for the church to be one, until that day when the steeples along Main Street no longer remind us of the scandal of our division but point together to the One who has been the source of our unity all along.

DISCUSSION QUESTIONS

1. Where do you see divisions between the Christians in your community? What are some things that keep us divided?

2. Why is unity important for Christians? Is unity even possible? Why or why not?

3. What are some challenges facing the churches today? How do they define our sense of mission?

4. Have you ever talked about your faith with a friend who goes to a different church than you? What did you talk about?

5. What are some ways that Christians can be united in spite of our differences?

NOTES

1. Lesslie Newbigin, *The Household of God: Lectures on the Nature of Church* (Eugene, OR: Wipf & Stock, 1953), 134.

2. The "1910 World Missionary Conference" was held in Edinburgh, Scotland. "Edinburgh 1910 Conference," Centenary of the 1910 World Missionary Conference, accessed April 23, 2013, http://www.edinburgh2010.org/en/resources/1910-conference.html.

3. "'Nones' on the Rise," *The Pew Forum on Religion and Public Life,* October 9, 2012, accessed April 23, 2013, http://www.pewforum.org/Unaffiliated/nones-on-the-rise.aspx.

4. "Letter to a Roman Catholic," in *John Wesley*, ed. Albert Outler (New York: Oxford University Press, 1964), 498.

5. Gayle Carlton Felton, *This Holy Mystery: A United Methodist Understanding of Holy Communion* (Nashville: Discipleship Resources, 2005), 57.

6. Lillian Daniel, "Spiritual but Not Religious? Please Stop Boring Me," *Huffington Post*, September 13, 2011, accessed April 23, 2013, http://www.huffingtonpost.com/lillian-daniel/spiritual-but-not-religio_b_959216.html.

7. "A Circle of Protection: A Statement on Why We Need to Protect Programs for the Poor," accessed April 23, 2013, http://www.circleofprotection.us/.

CHAPTER 6

"Who Is My Neighbor?"

Christian Identity and Interfaith Engagement

AWET ANDEMICHAEL

Loving Our Interfaith Neighbors

One day when I was five years old, I was sitting in the backseat of our family car miffed at my mother and my brother, seated on either side of me, for some affront I no longer remember. With all the drama and gravity I could muster, I wailed to my father: "How can I love my enemies when two of them are sitting right next to me?"

As Christians we are aware of Christ's call to love our neighbors, and to go even further and love our enemies. This has never been easy to do, but it seems even more difficult these days, as technology, trade, migration, and other globalizing forces shrink the world around us. Loving our neighbors was easier when they were mostly just like us. Loving our enemies was less challenging when we didn't have to interact with them in any significant way. But now we find ourselves confronting diversity on a daily basis.

Of the many kinds of diversity, religious difference is one of the most difficult to negotiate. For many of us, our religious identity is the core of our existence, the foundation on which all of our multiple identities and loyalties are built. Religion has been a factor in much conflict throughout history. Yet precisely because it is such an integral part of human life, religion is also a crucial force in peace building. Without peace and cooperation among people of different faiths, we are doomed to destroy ourselves and decimate the planet.

Yet how can we love our religious neighbors—genuinely love them—when their beliefs and practices place them at odds with us on the most basic level? Are we not betraying God and the Christian community when we fraternize too closely with people of other faiths? Won't we be tempted to water down or even betray our Christian beliefs and practices for the sake of interfaith harmony? Are we falling short of our Christian duty to spread the gospel when we fail to preach it at every possible opportunity? Will interreligious dialogue win us the world at the cost of our souls? Or is there a way to engage with people of other faiths that promotes a sustainable *shalom*—a peace for all peoples—without compromising our identities as followers of Christ?

I have no certain answers. I think of my close friends of different faiths and ideologies, and I know how deeply I love and am loved by them. But how often have we overlooked important differences, censored our remarks, or failed to share important parts of ourselves with one another for fear of causing offense or being rejected or misunderstood? I suppose these are the pitfalls in any relationship, but I am more conscious of them in interreligious ones, which require an extra measure of grace. As a Christian committed to interfaith dialogue but committed even more fundamentally to God in Christ Jesus through the Holy Spirit, I struggle to find the right balance.

One model for interreligious engagement seeks to identify areas of agreement and to use this theological common ground as a basis for bridge building. Much successful interdenominational and interfaith dialogue over the years has been conducted along these lines.[1] Yet as effective as this method has been in drawing people together across religious divides and in enriching self-understanding, its success is contingent on the very existence of some theological overlap between the faiths concerned. But what happens when there is little or no theological common ground of significance (for example, between theists and nontheists)? Or when groups come to similar conclusions but for diametrically opposed reasons (for example, that human life is of great value, because humans are created in the image of God, or because there is no god and therefore we can only rely on one another)? Do we call that true "common ground" or merely coincidental agreement?[2] Are we, as Christians, to relate only to those with whom we can find a common cause and dismiss the rest of our religious neighbors as beyond hope of reconciliation?

Another approach is to identify mutual interests and common social concerns. Various interreligious groups have expanded their mission to promote broader agendas for positive social change. They are committed to building up their communities and the world together. This is inevitably a complex process. Nurturing the unique religious identities of participants while creating space for them to grapple with the religious otherness of their partners in service is a messy process—as messy as real life. Differences inevitably come to the surface, raising challenging theological questions that can push participants far beyond their comfort zones. This dangerous, uncomfortable place is the only space in which profound learning and deep, sustainable transformation of relationships can occur. Yet without sufficient theological and diplomatic finesse, it holds the potential for the collapse of interfaith relations.

To protect against this danger, other interfaith coalitions for social action try to create a secular "neutral zone." Theological engagement, especially on any controversial questions, is avoided at all costs. Participants in this model are expected to "check religion at the door" and treat their interreligious partners as "just human beings." There may be situations so fraught with tension that only under such conditions can people of different faiths inhabit the same room, let alone work together. In general, however, I am troubled by this approach for two reasons. First,

I am suspicious of attempts to conceptualize religion as serving "greater ends" than God in God's glory. For Christians, at least, God is not a commodity, a "thing" among other things to be used to achieve human purposes—even laudable ones. While the wide range of possible interpretations of any religion makes it possible for peace-minded individuals to seek peace-oriented interpretations of their faith and religious practice, there always lurks the danger that we will extend our interpretive shaping to God, attempting to recreate God in a more peace-friendly image. Beginning with our dream of a perfect world, then stepping back to try to figure out what kind of a god would fit such a world, is far more likely to lead to idolatry than discovery of the true and living God.

Moreover, I am skeptical of the assumption that we are able truly to "check religion at the door." In today's world, we often struggle to master the feat of juggling multiple facets of our identities, even as we recognize the stable center that directs the act of juggling itself—the "me" who always remains "me." For people of faith, that center is shaped by and inextricably bound to our faith, practices, and beliefs. We can pretend to ignore the religious or ideological dimension of ourselves or find other ways to account for its influence on our actions and attitudes, but we are fooling ourselves if we think we can actually set it aside.

I cannot help but wonder: Could there be another way to approach the dilemma between Christian identity and interfaith dialogue? The more I think and pray about it, and meditate on Jesus' parable of the good Samaritan, the more hopeful I am. It seems to me that the key lies in asking the right question. Our primary challenge is not to ponder how we can manage our methods of interfaith engagement so as to minimize betraying who we are as Christians. Instead, our first and most fundamental task, the necessary foundation on which all subsequent steps depend, is to reexamine our very notion of *what it means to be Christian.*

What if we could reconcile identity and dialogue by basing our dialogue *in* our identity, rather than trying to downplay either side of the dialectic? When we understand our commitment to

Christ as being in opposition to, or in fundamental tension with, our commitment to interreligious engagement, we are, in effect, neglecting a critical aspect of Jesus' teachings. In the parable of the good Samaritan, Christ answers the question: "And who is my neighbor?" The story he tells teaches us to love our neighbor, to draw near to the one who seems furthest away, even when that distance is driven by religious difference. Thus, the very heart of what it means to be Christian—the "dual command" to love God and love our neighbor as ourselves (Luke 10:27)—gives us a solid basis for interreligious engagement in love.

A God-Given Starting Point

Jesus commands us: "Love your enemies, do good to those who hate you, bless those who curse you, pray for those who abuse you" (Luke 6:27-28). It sounds like an impossible command. It runs counter to the logic and moral symmetry of quid pro quo. It demands resources beyond what any human being can sustain. But in the words of Martin Luther King Jr., this command is "far from being the pious injunction of a utopian dreamer. . . . Jesus was very serious when he gave this command; he wasn't play-ing. . . . He realized that it was painfully hard, pressingly hard. But he wasn't playing."[3]

The starting point for faithful Christian interfaith engagement is God's relation to us. Christian theologies teach that even the widest theological distance between "us" and "them," whoever "we" or "they" may be, pales in comparison to the infinite distance between God and human beings. Yet these same Christian theologies also teach that God has come near to creation in "many and various ways" (Hebrews 1:1), offering the intimate breath of life at creation (Genesis 2:7); sustaining life by making the earth fruitful (Genesis 2:4-9); providing *torah*—God's life-giving instruction—as a handwritten gift to humanity through the people of Israel (Exodus 31:18); and even intervening to rescue those in danger (Psalms 78; 105). In Jesus Christ, God has come infinitely near to us in the divine self-disclosure that is Emmanuel ("God with us") and remains with us ("God as near") in the outpouring of the Holy Spirit.

The "us" to whom God has drawn near consists of the very enemies of God: we who have separated ourselves from the presence of God by our own sinfulness. God's grace to us is that, "while we still were sinners Christ died for us" (Romans 5:8). While we were still estranged, while the chasm was infinitely broad, while we were enemies of God (Romans 5:10), God chose to love us and, in that love, to reconcile us to Godself. This divine love, which reconciles us over an impossible distance, is the same love with which Christ calls us to love those who seem most distant from us.

In Christ, God has come near to us, so that we may come near to God. At the same time, this "nearness" to God grounds our loving approach to the distant neighbor. Thus, just like love in the famous "dual command" (Luke 10:27), nearness has both "vertical" and "horizontal" dimensions. If it were simply a question of utilizing God as a moral exemplar, then nearness would not be necessary.[4] But the key is the actual change wrought in our being by our drawing near to God. We cannot be in the presence of God without being affected. Only the one who has drawn near, who has *become* a child of God (see John 1:12; 1 John 3:1), can move beyond merely observing God's characteristics to striving to emulate those traits in our own lives.

The Unlikely Samaritan

Consider the parable of the man attacked by bandits on the way from Jerusalem to Jericho (Luke 10:25-37).[5] The first two people who encounter the half-dead man on the road pass by on the other side (Luke 10:31-32). Then the most unlikely of saviors comes along—a Samaritan traveler, an outsider, a person much more distant theologically speaking from the battered man (whom, we assume, is Jewish) than either of the previous passersby. Yet this seemingly dubious fellow, this "far" man, does something that neither the priest nor the Levite did: "[He] came near him; and when he saw him, he was moved with pity" (Luke 10:33).

Before we even read that the Samaritan *saw* the man in the road, we read that he "came near him," so that when he sees him, presumably he sees him from a position of nearness. The text indicates that he reacts differently from the priest and the Levite. We do not know if that difference came from their individual personalities, their cultural backgrounds, or other factors. We only know that the Samaritan "came near."

"And when he saw him, *he was moved with pity*" (Luke 10:33, italics added). Perhaps the Samaritan was a particularly devout and saintly person. Perhaps he was already deeply committed to Samaritan-Jewish dialogue or was a founding member of the Jericho Road Interfaith Safety Council! Or perhaps he was an ordinary human being with the twin impulses of prejudice and generosity tugging away within him. Regardless, it is clear that God worked in the heart of the Samaritan despite his socio-religious relationship to the battered man. Perhaps Jesus would have us regard the Samaritan as one who, in his drawing near, was also opening himself to the Holy Spirit—the Spirit who then moved him to compassion and enabled him to reach out to a neighbor in peril.

The Short Distance between Enemies and Neighbors

So this nearness is of a particular kind: an openness, a being-present-with, a seeing that sees and a hearing that hears. It is this nearness to which Christ calls us in our relationship with God. And it is through this nearness with one another that we enter a mode in which God's power can be unleashed for the accomplishment of *shalom*.

But notice how Christ goes about defining *nearness*. Clearly, more than spatial proximity is involved. The bandits, after all, had also come physically close to the Jewish traveler (v. 30). Rather, Jesus explains the term *neighbor* (literally, "the near one") as "the one who showed . . . mercy" (Luke 10:37), a definition that relates neither to physical proximity nor to identity of belief or culture. Jesus could have easily chosen a Jewish character to be the merciful one, but his actual choice serves to undermine the prevailing notion of *neighbor* in his time. By making a Samaritan the hero of a parable with an otherwise Jewish cast of characters, Christ's illustration of nearness explicitly crosses interfaith lines. In his exhortation to love the other, to "go and do likewise" (Luke 10:37), Christ thus reveals that we are to extend love-in-nearness not only to those within our religious circle, but specifically to those beyond it as well.

In the parable of the good Samaritan, Jesus expresses vividly the characteristics of such "near-one" love. The Samaritan could have simply shook his head in sympathy and passed by, which would have been more than the previous travelers had done. Or he could have hurried ahead to his destination to summon help. But the Samaritan, despite having every imaginable excuse *not* to do so, treated the battered Jewish stranger like a cherished family member, personally tending to his wounds, carrying him on his own animal to suitable accommodations, nursing him overnight, and footing his entire medical bill (Luke 10:34-35). The priest and Levite failed to see this man as their neighbor, not as evidenced by their actions, but by their failure to act.

Likewise, in the case of the command to "love your enemies," Jesus does not merely say, "Be neighborly" or "Let your interfaith neighbor know you care." He directs his listeners to counter enmity with specific acts of gracious love (Luke 6:27): confront hatred by doing good to the hater (Luke 6:27), counter cursing by blessing the curser (Luke 6:28), meet abuse with prayer for the abuser (Luke 6:28), and do not resist attacks on your person or your property (Luke 6:29-30)—in sum: to "love your enemies, do good, and lend, expecting nothing in return" (Luke 6:35).

Nearness and Distance in Today's Globalized World

Jesus' subversive definition of *neighbor* is particularly relevant to us in the context of twenty-first-century globalization. We might assume that in such an interconnected global community, lack of nearness is the least of our problems. We welcome, or complain about, immigrants and refugees in our midst. We purchase products from far afield. We access the thoughts and experiences of distant neighbors via the Internet and other media. We carry our mobile phones into remote deserts and wildernesses. The people with whom we interact in all these ways come from more and more disparate backgrounds. The person next door is becoming less and less likely to be "the one near"—whether culturally, ideologically, or religiously speaking.

But how do we tend to respond to the otherness that surrounds us? Do we retreat toward individualistic bubbles? Are we, as individuals and communities, shutting ourselves off, drifting further away—spiritually and emotionally—from the people in our midst, our neighbors? As Christians today we are called anew to follow the countercultural example of the Samaritan. We are called to collapse the distance between ourselves and our neighbors through acts of gracious love and hospitality. We are called to love our neighbors, not in spite of our differences, but precisely in the categories that caused us to define them as enemies in the first place. Christ chose a Samaritan as the hero of his tale, then extended the lesson to the Jewish lawyer, not the other way around. The religious otherness characterizing the relationship between the Samaritan and the presumably Jewish victim is a central feature of the parable, not an incidental detail that could have equally been otherwise. Likewise, the Samaritan makes no religious demands on the battered man, does not insist that he admit that the temple in Jerusalem is not the only valid place to worship God; nor does he declare his intention to convert to the Judaism of the Pharisees or Saduccees. The religious difference remains, and into that space of alienation and difference, the Samaritan pours love, concern, soothing oil, and nourishing food. In doing so, he and the battered man, and we and the religiously different people in our midst, experience the transformation of enemies into neighbors and come into new understandings of who we are as children of God in relationship to one another.

As Christians seeking interfaith reconciliation, we must be prepared to draw near—to move beyond dialogue in order to promote the *shalom* of people of other faiths as well as that of our own coreligionists. But what about spreading the Christian faith and defending it against the "enemies of God"? Will our impulse to share the good news of Jesus become muffled by our attempts to maintain diplomatic restraint in dealing with people of other faiths? These are indeed challenging dilemmas for which there are no easy answers. But when we "draw near," we must do so because God has called us to do this in all our interactions, and *not* primarily as an effective operational strategy for evangelization. Whether, in a particular situation, we share our faith explicitly with others or not, we are always called to "draw near" in active love, in whatever capacity we can. If we witness to our faith in word as well as deed, as led by the Spirit, then we have the assurance that the same Spirit who inspires us also works in the hearts of those who hear our witness. And if we believe that God's own Spirit touches people's hearts and brings them to *shalom*, as we understand it, and that our own efforts are crucial but not ultimate factors in this process, then this may introduce a godly element of humility to our evangelizing.

A similar sort of humility would serve us well in our efforts to defend the faith. As Christians, we must distinguish between the defense of Christianity as a religion and the defense of God, Godself. It is appropriate to explain Christianity in a sympathetic light, to strengthen the understanding and revitalize the practice of the faith, and to define clearly the differences between Christianity and other religions. In fact, the practice of apologetics is not only important but is necessary for the flourishing of Christianity. But attempts to defend God's honor, while probably well-intentioned, are fundamentally unnecessary. It is inconsistent to regard God as omnipotent and not at all contingent on creation, yet at the same time deem God as vulnerable to attack from a created power. As Mamma Etaghegnehu, an elderly family friend with no formal education, wisely cautioned my mother, "Do not worry about defending God: God will defend himself."

In the final analysis, we are not making peace with our neighbor's god or beliefs. We are making peace with our *neighbor*. But we are doing so without evading her otherness or separating her from her distinct religious identity, or falling into this trap ourselves. Yet if our impulse to love our neighbor of another faith or ideology is not fostered by a conviction deeply rooted in our own religious beliefs, then we are setting ourselves up for an inevitable conflict between our identity as Christians and our desire for interfaith peace. It is for these reasons that I believe that authentic dialogue, firmly grounded in the rich theological resources from each tradition, is the best foundation for effective interfaith engagement.

We are called to follow Christ, and this requires Spirit-led, action-oriented love of our fellow human beings, including especially people of other faiths. Faithfulness to God and love of our religious neighbors are not necessarily competing goals but, rather, complex demands of Christian identity and Christian love. It is when we fail to recognize this that we settle, by omission or commission, for compromised solutions based on fear and not faith. It is when we define our Christian identity as one construction of self among others, rather than a complete and humbling transformation in the presence of the living God, that we choose the either/or path, the simplification we can grasp and control.

Let us trust in God's transformative love, in Christ's enabling command, in the Spirit's continual assistance in our task. Let us remember that we, as today's Samaritans, are proximate ambassadors at best—in the service of the Most High God. For even as we approach in love the beaten and bruised along today's roadways, we carry with us our identity as those who are also bruised and battered yet rescued, restored, healed, and saved by our Great Samaritan. Let us strive to be faithful witnesses of the gospel in our lives and actions, trusting in the Holy Spirit to touch the hearts of all those whom God places in our path.

DISCUSSION QUESTIONS

1. Does your faith in Christ compel you to reach out to those of different faiths? Why or why not?

2. What are the various models of interfaith engagement that you have encountered? What are the pros and cons of each model?

3. What do you think is (or would be) the most effective model for interfaith engagement?

4. Who are your religious neighbors? What opportunities do you see to draw nearer to them?

5. What other theological or biblical resources can you think of that might be useful for thinking about interreligious engagement?

NOTES

1. The Evangelical Lutheran Church in America (ELCA), for example, has established full communion or bilateral conversations with a wide range of Christian and non-Christian communities. "Ecumenical and Inter-Religious Relations," Evangelical Lutheran Church in America, accessed April 23, 2013, http://www.elca.org/ecumenical. Another example is the "Common Word" Initiative for Christian-Muslim dialogue. Miroslav Volf, Ghazi bin Muhammad, and Melissa Yarrington, eds., *A Common Word: Muslims and Christians on Loving God and Neighbor* (Grand Rapids: Eerdmans, 2010).

2. One critic of this approach was American Orthodox Rabbi Joseph B. Soloveitchik (1903–1993): "Each faith community is engaged in a singular normative gesture reflecting the numinous nature of the act of faith itself, and it is futile to try to find common denominators." Joseph Soloveitchik, "Confrontation," *Tradition* 6, no. 2 (1964):19; quoted in Daniel Rynhold, "The Philosophical Foundations of Soloveitchik's Critique of Interfaith Dialogue," *Harvard Theological Review* 96, no. 1 (2003): 104.

3. Martin Luther King Jr., "Loving your Enemies" (sermon, Dexter Avenue Baptist Church, Montgomery, AL, November 17, 1957), http://www.love yourenemies.org/mlking.html.

4. The theme of "nearness" pervades this section of the Lukan gospel account. In chapter 10, when Christ commissions the Seventy to preach the gospel, the message he gives them to declare is: "The kingdom of God has *come near*" (v. 11, italics added). Immediately following the parable, in the story of Jesus' visit to Martha and Mary, Jesus commends Mary for drawing near to him—literally, sitting "at the Lord's feet" and listening to what he says (v. 39).

5. See Gustavo Gutiérrez, *A Theology of Liberation*, 2nd ed. (Maryknoll, NY: Orbis, 1988), 113–16; and Scott Dolff, "Mercy, Human and Divine" (PhD diss., Yale University, 2009), 96–119.

PART TWO

Renewing Hope for the Church's Witness Today and into the Future

CHAPTER 7

Stewards of Creation

A Christian Calling for Today's Ecological Crisis

IAN S. MEVORACH

Indeed Very Good

In the first chapter of the Bible, after God creates the heavens and the earth, the Scripture says, "God saw everything that he had made, and indeed, it was *very good*" (Genesis 1:31, italics added). Up until that point, a slightly different phrase—"God saw that it was good"—is repeated again and again, the refrain of the creation story (Genesis 1:4,10,12,18,21,25). But it is not until the last act of creation, when God creates humanity in God's own image and likeness, that we hear that everything is not just good, but "*very good.*" The foundational story of the Bible, then, affirms humanity as a uniquely important and valuable part of God's creation. Made in the image of God, we are the stewards and caretakers of creation. As such, we are charged with the responsibility to conserve and protect the earth. We are called to mirror God's love and care for creation by living in such a way that our lives magnify its goodness.

When one looks upon the natural world today and sees the clear signs of the ecological crisis—species extinction, masses of garbage, polluted waters, and strange weather—the idea of humanity adding to the goodness and beauty of creation seems out of touch with reality. Possibly in my lifetime, and certainly in that of my children and grandchildren, coastal cities I have visited or lived in may be underwater, plants and animals that existed in abundance may be scarce or extinct, and the world's rain forests may be cleared and its coral reefs dead. All of this foreboding devastation can be linked directly to irresponsible human activities. As Christians we are called to live on this earth in a way that is a blessing, not a curse, for our own and future generations. We are called to be God's people who ensure that creation is not only good, but indeed *very good*.

Though I grew up in the church, my entry point into becoming a follower of Jesus was a copy of the New Testament that I received from a group of Gideons during orientation week at Middlebury College, a liberal arts college in the Green Mountains of Vermont. There I discovered that the Jesus of the Gospels was (and is) simply magnetic to me. Thus began my transition from a "spiritual but not religious" teenager on the way out of Christianity to a young adult with an irresistible call to live my life in the way of Jesus. At the same time as my Christian faith was awakening, I also began to frequent the Weybridge House, an alternative house on the edge of campus where students prepared their meals from scratch using local and organic ingredients. Besides the conscientiously made, delicious food, I also appreciated the sense of warmth and community I found there. Eating at the Weybridge House and joining in charged dinner conversations about transforming our society and healing the earth, I was quickly becoming an environmentalist.

In hindsight it is easy for me to see how these two major pieces of my life came together—that is, Christian discipleship and environmentalism. The connection is right there in the first chapter of the Bible, a connection I discovered in my studies of the life and work of Martin Luther King Jr. while in seminary at Boston University School of Theology. I intentionally chose to attend Boston

University because King studied for his doctorate there. In my first year, I joined the American Baptist Churches USA, as King himself was Baptist. In general, he has been very influential in the way I have understood and responded to my call to ministry. What I find in King, and in the churches that supported the civil rights movement, is a vital connection between heaven and earth, a point at which Christianity and the gospel become relevant and transform the world. As I have grown in my commitments—as a follower of Jesus, student of King, and environmentalist, I have become aware of how deeply intertwined the Christian, civil rights, and environmental movements are, or at least can be.

The Church as Thermostat

In 1963, locked in a jail cell in Birmingham, Alabama, Martin Luther King Jr. wrote powerfully about the church's failure to challenge the institutionalized racial injustice of segregation. Without losing their original force, these words apply today to the church's failure to stand up with all people of faith and conscience against humanity's crimes against creation.

> There was a time when the church was very powerful—in the time when the early Christians rejoiced at being deemed worthy to suffer for what they believed. In those days the church was not merely a thermometer that recorded the ideas and principles of popular opinion; it was a thermostat that transformed the mores of society. . . . If today's church does not recapture the sacrificial spirit of the early church, it will lose its authenticity, forfeit the loyalty of millions, and be dismissed as an irrelevant social club with no meaning.[1]

King's comparison of the church of his times to a thermometer rather than a thermostat is especially poignant when we consider the church's role in the ecological crisis. At the center of this crisis, of course, is the problem of global warming, the overheating of our planet caused by excessive consumption of fossil fuels. More than ever before, Christians need to rediscover our role as a thermostat that can transform our society and quite literally turn the temperature down before we destroy our planet. If the church fails to challenge the status quo—which has brought about climate change, habitat destruction, species extinction, and pollution of air, water, and land—it will lose its legitimacy as a moral compass for rising generations.

Many Christians are becoming more aware of the ecological crisis and remembering their role as stewards of creation. Theologians are writing books on the subject, and churches are taking action, from switching from Styrofoam coffee cups to ceramic mugs, to practicing composting and putting solar panels on their buildings. We are remembering and honoring the lives of Saints such as Francis of Assisi, who lived simply and showed compassion for the earth and all creatures. These are all important steps in the right direction. However, the Christian community's engagement with this crisis must go beyond the steadily shrinking cultural and physical space we call "church." We must seek to transform our society by expanding our concept of the sacred space in which we are called to *be church*—the sacred space that is all of creation. As Scripture says, "The earth is the LORD's and all that is in it" (Psalm 24:1). In the twenty-first century, churches must directly and forcefully challenge the injustices in our world, including the exploitation of the earth and its creatures, just as if this exploitation were occurring in our sanctuaries on Sunday morning.

Christianity and the Environmental Movement

In February 2013 I attended the largest climate justice rally in US history. More than forty thousand people gathered in Washington, DC to pressure President Obama and his administration to "Move Forward on Climate." The principal organization behind this rally was 350.org, which was cofounded by environmental author and activist Bill McKibben and several Middlebury College students who lived at the Weybridge House from 2005 to 2007. Inspired by McKibben's work in his capacity as "scholar in residence," these students had organized effective campaigns to overhaul the college's strategies for energy consumption and production, and in general to make climate change an issue on campus and beyond. Standing by the Washington Monument in a throng of activists that day, I was amazed at the movement that had grown out of the commitment to the earth formed around the simplicity of wholesome meals and good company at the Weybridge House.

The rally was emceed by Rev. Lennox Yearwood, president and CEO of the Hip Hop Caucus, a national organization that seeks to "mobilize, educate, and engage young people, ages 14 to 40, on the social issues that directly impact their lives and communities."[2] Under Yearwood's leadership, the Hip Hop Caucus engages young people, especially people of color, in a number of important political movements under the umbrellas of "Civil and Human Rights" and "Environmental Justice and Climate." From my vantage point, amid a predominantly white crowd of environmental activists at this rally, the leaders of color on the stage (including African Americans, Native Americans, and Hispanics) signified both the reality of the racial divide within the movement and a desire for a more inclusive way forward.

Many white environmentalists joined the fight against climate change after reading scientific studies and considering the issue rather abstractly. This is illustrated by the name 350.org—a reference to the parts per million of carbon dioxide in the atmosphere, which climate scientists have indicated is the maximum for sustaining life as we know it on earth. (Currently we're well above that maximum, at 392 ppm carbon dioxide in the atmosphere.) However, many people of color have joined the environmental justice movement based on their social and political experiences. The story of the Hip Hop Caucus is a clear example:

> The Hip Hop Caucus has been aligned with the environmental movement since 2005 when we were working on the ground in the Gulf Coast and in Washington DC to fight for a fair and just response to the destruction caused by Hurricane Katrina. No moment

has so clearly shown the world who suffers first and worst—the poor and people of color—from the devastation of natural disasters caused by extreme weather patterns, which are increasing because of global warming.[3]

Whereas 350.org seeks to raise awareness about climate change through education about the problem of excess carbon dioxide in the atmosphere, the Hip Hop Caucus "creat[es] materials and resources that illustrate how environmental issues impact the daily lives of people of color, with a particular focus on health impacts of pollution, the same pollution that comes from extracting and burning fossil fuels that are causing climate change."[4] Many poor people and people of color live in communities where environmental issues pose an immediate threat to their health and well-being. For these communities, the future effects of carbon emissions are of lesser concern than the current side-effects of living in areas of heavy pollution, such as high rates of asthma. In order for the environmental movement to become a popular movement with the power to achieve substantial social change, its platform and scope must widen dramatically to include both the current *and* future impacts of the environmental crisis, as well as an analysis and dismantling of systems of structural racism.

This is not a new challenge, to be sure. Churches and other communities of faith, because of their concern for justice for the poor, have long been at the forefront of this work.[5] In 1982, for example, the United Church of Christ's Commission on Racial Justice set out to study the issue after helping to organize protests against the location of a toxic waste site in predominately African American Warren County, North Carolina. Rev. Benjamin F. Chavis Jr., a leader of the protests and one of the principal authors of the commission's 1987 report titled "Toxic Wastes and Race in the United States," is widely credited with coining the term *environmental racism*.[6] The report identified race as the most significant statistical indicator of where hazardous waste sites are located in the United States; that is, such sites are disproportionately found where African Americans, Native Americans, and other people of color reside.[7]

In direct response to the problem of environmental racism, the environmental *justice* movement emerged in the late 1980s. Leaders of the environmental justice movement—primarily people of color, many of them clergy—are not willing to rank human concerns behind more abstract environmental ones. They focus mainly on issues such as pollution in cities and unsafe conditions for farm workers. In other words, they are concerned with issues that daily and directly affect the populations they represent.[8] At a meeting with the executive directors of the Sierra Club and the Natural Resources Defense Council, black activist Dana Alston succinctly stated the challenge that environmental justice brings to mainstream environmentalism: "Our vision of the environment is woven into an overall framework of social, racial, and economic justice."[9]

An Inclusive Approach to the Climate Crisis

Martin Luther King Jr. modeled an inclusive approach to social activism that is instructive for giving Christian witness to today's climate crisis. He started off focusing on the issue of racial equality. However, he soon branched out to advocate for economic justice and workers' rights. After that he protested against the Vietnam War. King's leadership demonstrated his profound understanding that "injustice anywhere is a threat to justice everywhere."[10] He did not focus solely on one issue, limited to his own personal experiences; his outlook was inclusive of the experiences of others. He made connections among justice issues in the United States and understood the US-based movement for peace and justice as part of a global revolution.

In his compelling remarks during the "Forward on Climate" rally, Yearwood noted the fact that it coincided with the fifty-year anniversary of the March on Washington for Jobs and Freedom. One remarkable aspect of that march was that King and other leaders brought together two apparently distinct issues—civil and economic rights—in a creative synthesis, thereby unifying blacks and whites. Seeing Yearwood, a protégé of King, leading the largest climate rally in US history, gave me hope that this movement is headed toward such a creative and unifying synthesis of issues.

Of course, much work remains ahead. In conversations with activists of color after the rally at the first People's Assembly on the Climate Crisis, I heard loud and clear that the climate movement needs to be more intentional about inclusivity—in leadership, setting the agenda, and galvanizing the movement. Uniting the movement across the racial divide will require the strengthening of relationships between climate activists and environmental justice activists, and ensuring that issues such as poverty, access to quality education, healthcare, employment, and housing are central on the climate crisis agenda.[11]

Doing God's Will on Earth

When Jesus' students asked him how to pray, he told them to say, "Your kingdom come. Your will be done, on earth as it is in heaven" (Matthew 6:10). For as much as Jesus talked about the future and the life beyond this world, he cared deeply about life on earth. Jesus was a healer. Jesus gave bread to the hungry. He fought for justice and spoke the truth about the abuses of the powerful. For Jesus the "kingdom of God" was not so much another world that would descend out of the sky as it was God's will done on earth. To follow Jesus today, and to belong to the church that calls him Lord, is to strive to live one's life on earth according to God's will. This is no small challenge.

In a society that idolizes money, we are called to live by the maxim "You cannot serve God and wealth" (Matthew 6:24). By our words and deeds, we are called to challenge the assumption that any new way we conceive of to exploit and consume the earth's natural goods is acceptable, so long as it makes money in the short term. If every person of faith and good conscience were to repent of our nation's worship of money and instead start serving God, our culture of unsustainable consumption would shift radically. Imagine a world where *sufficiency* or *need* is the norm governing what and how we buy and sell, rather than *want* or *greed*. Entire industries would vanish, including the most highly polluting industries that support war, violence, and oppression worldwide. People would live frugally, sharing the necessities of life, relying more on local resources from the natural environment, and cultivating awareness of the sacredness of each other and all life. This world is possible, and it is necessary. The role of the churches is to compellingly articulate our faith in the Creator and to model and shape the attitudes and practices that will call us back to our God-given role as stewards of creation.

A Crisis-Packed Calling

Churches and other faith communities, joining forces with environmentalists and people of conscience, can and should stage a concerted resistance to the destruction of the natural world. In his "Letter from Birmingham Jail," King described the strategy and philosophy of nonviolent resistance to evil, which he adapted from the philosophy of Gandhi. He named the four steps for any campaign of nonviolent resistance: fact-gathering, self-purification, negotiation, and direct action.[12] For the most part, these are precisely the steps that environmental activists have taken. Time and again they have gathered the facts. They have purified themselves by changing their own lifestyles according to those facts and by committing to take social and political action. In most cases they have found that corporations and governments are unwilling to negotiate in keeping with these facts, and so they have repeatedly organized direct action—whether marches, sit-ins, or demonstrations in the way of destructive building or mining projects.

In his jail cell in Birmingham in 1963, King laid out the rationale for his direct action campaign against racial injustice in that city against detractors from among the local clergy who accused him of causing agitation and disruption.

> Nonviolent direct action seeks to create such a crisis and foster such a tension that a community which has constantly refused to negotiate is forced to confront the issue. It seeks to so dramatize the issue

so that it can no longer be ignored. . . . The purpose of our direct action program is to create a situation so crisis-packed that it will inevitably open the door to negotiation.[13]

If we take our roles as stewards of creation seriously, then I believe that we need to join our hearts, minds, souls, and bodies in a campaign of nonviolent resistance against corporations and governments who refuse to change economic practices. As we engage in this campaign, we must work intentionally as churches to overcome the racism that continues to divide, not only the environmental movement, but our churches themselves. It would be a beautiful sight to see Christians of all colors standing together with others for environmental and climate justice. With our bodies and souls on the line, literally blocking the way of ecological destruction, we would stand not only as stewards of creation seeking justice for the earth, but as children of God seeking reconciliation and unity for the human family.

We read in the Gospel of Luke that on a certain occasion Jesus accepted an invitation to eat dinner at a Pharisee's house (Luke 11:37). In the midst of this dinner, violating all the norms of polite conversation, Jesus accused his hosts of being "full of greed and wickedness" (Luke 11:39). I believe that his words were commensurate with the problems he was speaking to—the violence and oppression of his society's ruling elite. This is the kind of bold attitude we must have to break through the facades that paper over the major injustices of our day.

When dealing with an issue as catastrophic and pressing as the ecological crisis, we need to break the rules of polite conversation. We need to put aside the conventional methods of assigning responsibility that never seem to pin it down on anyone with money or power. We need to speak truth to the weak and the powerful alike based on the facts at hand and make denial of the problem simply impossible. As King so eloquently stated, we need "to create a situation so crisis-packed that it will inevitably open the door to negotiation."[14] This is our calling in today's ecological crisis. How will we respond?

DISCUSSION QUESTIONS

1. Would you consider the ecological crisis a religious issue? Why or why not?

2. What passages of Scripture or religious practices strengthen your belief in God as Creator?

3. Would you consider your lifestyle sustainable? Why or why not? In what ways (if any) have you considered making changes to your lifestyle?

4. Have you ever witnessed or participated in a campaign of nonviolent resistance? If yes, how do you see this participation in relationship to your faith?

5. What connections do you see between the civil rights movement and the environmental movement?

NOTES

1. Martin Luther King Jr., "Letter from Birmingham Jail" (letter, Birmingham, AL, April 16, 1963) http://mlk-kpp01.stanford.edu/index.php/resources/article/annotated_letter_from_birmingham/.

2. "Mission Statement," Hip Hop Caucus, accessed April 23, 2013, http://www.hiphopcaucus.org/company/.

3. "Environmental Justice and Climate Change," Hip Hop Caucus, accessed April 23, 2013, http://www.hiphopcaucus.org/environmental-justice-and-climate-change/index.php.

4. Ibid.

5. Since the 1970s, the World Council of Churches, a global fellowship of churches, has been praying and advocating for "Justice, Peace, and Integrity of Creation"—not as isolated goals, but as integral parts of the world we hope for by faith. "The WCC and Eco-Justice," World Council of Churches, accessed April 23, 2013, http://www.oikoumene.org/en/what-we-do/eco-justice.

6. See Marguerite L. Spencer, "Environmental Racism and Black Theology: James H. Cone Instructs Us on Witness," *University of St. Thomas Law Journal* 290, vol. 5:1 (2008), http://ir.stthomas.edu/cgi/viewcontent.cgi?article=1144&context=ustlj; and "Toxic Wastes and Race in the United States: A National Report on the Racial and Socio-Economic Characteristics of Communities with Hazardous Waste Sites," Commission for Racial Justice, United Church of Christ, 1987, accessed April 23, 2013, http://www.ucc.org/about-us/archives/pdfs/toxwrace87.pdf.

7. Vernice Miller-Travis, "Social Transformation through Environmental Justice," in *Christianity and Ecology*, ed. Dieter T. Hessel and Rosemary Radford Ruether (Cambridge: Harvard University Press for the Center for the Study of World Religions, 2000), 562.

8. Martin V. Melosi, "Environmental Justice, Ecoracism, and Environmental History," in *To Love the Wind and the Rain: African Americans and Environmental History*, ed. Dianne D. Glave and Mark Stoll (Pittsburgh: University of Pittsburgh Press, 2006), 124.

9. Dana Alston, quoted in Mark Stoll, "Religion and African American Environmental Activism," in *To Love the Wind and the Rain*, ed. Glave and Stoll, 150–51.

10. King, "Letter from Birmingham Jail."

11. "Notes from First Meeting," People's Assembly on the Climate Crisis, February 17, 2013, accessed April 23, 2013, http://www.bostonclimateresearch.com/uploads/Peoples_Assembly_Report_of_17_February_2013_g.pdf, 8–10.

12. King, "Letter from Birmingham Jail."

13. Ibid.

14. Ibid.

CHAPTER 8

Toward a Fuller Hospitality

The Church and
Intellectual Disability

ERINN STALEY

Seeking a Church Home

My friend Victoria is preparing to be confirmed. Late on a Sunday evening, she will gather with her regular worship community, a campus ministry located twenty-five miles from her home. The community will hold its final student Mass of the semester, and those who have spent much of the year prayerfully exploring their faith will experience this special rite of initiation into the Christian church.

I am excited for my friend, who is eager to have her membership in the church recognized and celebrated. For her, confirmation has been a long time coming. Before Victoria found a home in her campus ministry community, other churches failed to welcome her because she has developmental disabilities. One priest doubted her fitness for confirmation, asking, "Does she really know God?"

The discrimination that Victoria experienced is all too common. Congregations that intentionally and meaningfully include intellectually disabled people are the exception rather than the rule.[1] While some experiences of exclusion are overt, most are subtle. Unwelcome is communicated through a range of behaviors, including not being invited to attend, being asked *not* to attend, and being allowed to attend but not welcome to participate fully in worship and other aspects of church life, such as confirmation or the Eucharist. Yet the church, as a community of Christ, is called to a fuller hospitality than this.

Respecting Human Dignity

Brett Webb-Mitchell, who has written several books about the church and intellectual disability, reports: "People with disabilities and their families tell countless stories of being politely asked to leave worship, or in some cases of being *told* not to come to church, with comments such as, 'I don't think this is a church where you and your family would feel comfortable.'"[2] Such comments, which claim to express concern for the comfort of intellectually disabled people and their families, often have more to do with nondisabled churchgoers' discomfort with disability.

The exclusion of intellectually disabled people from the church fails to recognize their full dignity as human beings. Familiar ways of characterizing what it means to be human center on being able to think and to do certain things, such as make decisions about the direction of one's life. These views about what it means to be fully a human being have roots in theological and philosophical characterizations of humanity that emphasize rationality or other capacities for reflection and action.

In recent centuries, privileging rational capacities as definitive of what it means to be human has been used to exclude various groups of marginalized people, including women and people of color, from civil rights, public leadership, and institutions including the church. In response, these groups demonstrated their capacity to conform to normative standards of rationality, gaining improved status in society and the church. Since rational capacities are diminished in or absent from intellectually disabled people, however, prevailing ways of talking about what it is to be human undermine their claim to full personhood.

While churchgoers or pastors might not self-consciously reflect on these connections, I suggest that this privileging of rationality undergirds negative attitudes toward disabled people in the church and ambivalence about whether they can be Christian. Presumably it is these kinds of assumptions that influenced the thinking of the priest who doubted my friend's ability to have knowledge of God, as well as other church leaders who have prohibited intellectually disabled people from attending worship, being baptized, or receiving the Eucharist. Helping churches to move from discriminating against intellectually disabled people to offering them hospitality means helping churches to affirm the full humanity of people with intellectual disabilities. Indeed, God relates creatively to all human beings, loving us into being and giving us value, which we are called to recognize and honor in one another. No human being is endowed with the power to create herself, to elicit God's love, or to know God fully. Rather, all people, regardless of ability, are radically dependent on God for our very existence and for bestowing us with dignity.[3]

When the church fails to embrace the fullness of human beings, the church fails to embrace its own fullness. In other words, when a congregation excludes an intellectually disabled person and fails to honor that person's dignity, it also misses out on the God-given gifts that individual would have shared with the church. The Spirit bestows diverse gifts on people for the good of the community, and when a person is absent, the church lacks her particular contributions. It does not cease to be the church, but it less fully exemplifies what God calls and equips it to be.

While talk of "ministry" often emphasizes the vocational work of ordained clergy, fundamentally ministry refers to the work to which God calls *all* Christians. While all are called to ministry, all are not called to or equipped for the same forms of ministry. For this reason, engaging in ministry first involves communal discernment and embrace of individuals' particular gifts. In the words of the World Council of Churches' statement on Baptism, Eucharist and Ministry:

> The Holy Spirit bestows on the community diverse and complementary gifts. These are for the common good of the whole people and are manifested in acts of service within the community and to the world. They may be gifts of communicating the Gospel in word and deed, gifts of healing, gifts of praying, gifts of teaching and learning, gifts of serving, gifts of guiding and following, gifts of inspiration and vision. All members are called to discover, with the help of the community, the gifts they have received and to use them for the building up of the Church and for the service of the world to which the Church is sent.[4]

My friend Victoria, for instance, has received God's gift for welcoming others. Wherever she goes, she introduces herself, asks the names of the people she meets, and remembers them. She inquires about people's loved ones and asks after their well-being. The churches that have fallen short of welcoming Victoria in the past have missed an opportunity to embrace her and to benefit from the welcome she would have shared with the community. Having visited churches of various traditions over many years, I have noticed that not all congregations are sufficiently gifted for welcome, although welcome is key to the church's work of hospitality. Oftentimes a newcomer or visitor may be greeted in a cursory fashion or not at all. These congregations would be more welcoming, joyful places—fuller instantiations of the church—if they had more members gifted for welcome. I give thanks that my friend Victoria is being confirmed, both because including her in the rite affirms her dignity and because I can see how much the church needs her gifts.

To be clear, I am not suggesting that all intellectually disabled people are gifted in this way. The reason the church needs Victoria is because the Spirit has bestowed particular gifts on her as an individual. Indeed, we all can strive to participate in and support the multiple works to which the church is called, and we do this best when we collectively discern and affirm the presence of special gifts, whether for welcoming, praying, preaching, teaching, or some other calling, in each person.

When a congregation takes the time to get to know an intellectually disabled person, rather than viewing his presence as a problem, it can learn how to support his well-being and help discern the ways the Spirit equips him for the good of the community. As churches move from discriminating against intellectually disabled people to welcoming them, it is especially important to attend to discerning their gifts. I hope, moreover, that congregations that seek with renewed enthusiasm to discern members' gifts will discover and embrace gifts that have been overlooked among nondisabled as well as disabled people. Certainly all of us have received gifts from God for the good of the community.

Imagining Inclusion through the Metaphor of the Body of Christ

Nondisabled churchgoers might desire to welcome disabled people into the life of the congregation. At the same time, they might feel unable to reconcile the idea of an intellectually disabled person being baptized or receiving the Eucharist with what they think it means to be Christian—to choose to believe certain things about Jesus Christ, to pray, to make responsible ethical choices, and so on. If an intellectually disabled person whose experiences of reflecting, choosing, and acting seem different or nonexistent can be Christian, then what does this mean for nondisabled people? Is it not important and meaningful to think critically about God, to choose certain beliefs or actions deliberately? When nondisabled Christians take seriously the possibility that intellectually disabled people really can be Christian too, this may prompt an identity crisis. What does it mean, in light of these differences, to be Christian? I propose that when congregations experience this tension, they need not abandon their view of Christian life in order to be inclusive of disabled people. Instead, this view can expand as their practices become more inclusive.

Congregations can begin to improve their welcome and inclusion of intellectually disabled people by reflecting on the metaphor of the church as the body of Christ, which has a biblical origin and is familiar to contemporary churchgoers as an expression of the universal church and the unity of Christians. The metaphor of the body might seem a surprising basis on which to encourage the inclusion of disabled people, whose bodies and minds often differ from cultural norms. However, I think it is a helpful affirmation that bodies matter; in other words, to use the body as a metaphor relies on the reality of bodies rather than providing a way to say that bodies are just metaphors—and it suggests that Christians ought not shy away from talking about and caring for bodies in all their diversity.

Most importantly, the unity that the image of the body represents is not uniformity, because the members of the body are diverse and possess different gifts. This diversity is *essential* to the flourishing of the body, not a characteristic that exists *despite* the unity of the body. Put differently, to be a body necessarily is to be a connection of many and varied parts, not to be a connection of many identical parts. It also is instructive that the many and varied parts of the church body are innumerable rather than being a checklist (one preacher, two prophets, two teachers, and so on) that could be used to reinforce cultural norms of human bodies (two arms of a certain type, two legs of a certain type, and so on). As churches continue to seek and embrace the spiritual gifts that constitute the body of Christ and contribute to its flourishing, so may churches begin to imagine and work to incorporate diverse literal bodies as full members of the church.

Practicing Hospitality

Notions such as hospitality quickly lose meaning if they are not attached to concrete practices, but it is not always obvious what steps a Christian community might take to move toward a goal. When a congregation considers who is missing from its community and discerns a call to reach out to those who are not yet included meaningfully, how might it begin to extend hospitality? True welcome of intellectually disabled people involves inviting them in rather than simply observing that there seem not to be any intellectually disabled people in one's church. It means providing support such as transportation to make accepting an invitation possible and welcoming people who attend without imposing norms of conduct on them, such as expecting them to sit still and be silent for significant periods of time, that may be at odds with their impairments.

A common concern among nondisabled people is that intellectually disabled people will be disruptive in church, and this worry will not be overcome easily. One parent of a child with special needs writes that after ushers tried to make her son sit in the back of the sanctuary, "I haven't been going to church at all because apparently we are a nuisance to the other people in church, which makes me REALLY sad. . . . Going to a restaurant is also an extreme challenge, so we RARELY do that. However, no one at [the restaurant] tells us that we need to change our table or sit at separate tables because our son is disruptive."[5] Becoming more hospitable will require the church to do more than give intellectually disabled people a chance to prove that they can assimilate to the norms for behavior in worship.

Further, hospitality means more than inviting intellectually disabled people to have a separate worship service.[6] Rather than creating segregated worship services, hospitality means doing some things differently in the main worship setting, such as creating more opportunities for movement and noise. A mark of an inclusive community is its willingness to change in response to its members rather than making conformity a condition of entrance into the community. As one hospitable churchgoer assured a mother of a child with autism, "If we're doing our job right as a church . . . you and your son will always feel at home here. No matter what."[7]

Many churchgoers hold dear certain worship practices and traditions, and it is not necessary to abandon those in order to become more inclusive (although it likely will be important to modify some of them). When a congregation considers what adaptations it might make, it can look to the principles that already guide its worship, such as praise or togetherness, and consider how to extend them in relation to intellectually disabled people. Churches rooted in different traditions and styles will find a range of opportunities to make people feel at home that differ according to a community's priorities, such as capitalizing on an emphasis on music, small groups, or sharing meals together.

The most common stories of discrimination against intellectually disabled people in the church involve disruption, or the threat of disruption, in worship or Sunday school. For this reason, efforts to provide hospitality to intellectually disabled people must begin with worship and Christian education, but they must not end there. True inclusion of intellectually disabled people in the community means not simply nondisabled people accepting their presence, but cultivating authentic relationships with them. Building such relationships can draw on many of the same practices of outreach and kindness to which welcoming churches already are committed, such as greeting strangers during the passing of the peace, inviting them to coffee hour or lunch after worship, and making conversation about shared interests or hobbies.

A further sign that an intellectually disabled person truly has been welcomed into and included in a community will be when she becomes not only a recipient of its hospitality but a contributor to its ministries, in whatever ways she is capacitated and called. Just as nondisabled members of the community are both recipients and practitioners of hospitality, both ministered to and ministering to others, so too will intellectually disabled people who are thoroughly part of the community both receive and offer welcome and care.

Remembering God's Graciousness

Finally, when congregations struggle with whether and how to include intellectually disabled people in the life of the church, we would do well to keep our focus on God's graciousness to humanity rather than on human capacities or actions. I already have suggested that looking to God's loving, creative relationship to all human beings can help churches affirm the full human dignity of intellectually disabled people. Likewise, focusing on God's graciousness in any human experience or knowledge of God, including in practices such as baptism, Eucharist, and confirmation, can help alleviate concerns about whether any individual "can really know God." Christians widely affirm that the Eucharist is a mystery, and surely it is disingenuous to suggest that anyone, however intelligent or pious, truly understands its meaning. Similarly, there are profound limits to human understanding of God's gracious presence to us in private prayer, corporate worship, or other experiences.

While it is good to contemplate God's gracious presence, however one is able to do so, we ought not mistake this practice with mastering grace. We dare not suppose that God's love for us is contingent on our comprehending it sufficiently. Recognizing the profound difference between humanity and God, I would reframe the concern about whether an intellectually disabled person "can really know God" to acknowledge the limits of what any human being can know of God. Whatever knowledge we do have, however partial, certainly is a gift. Human beings are diverse in a host of ways that are worth affirming, but in our radical dependence on God's grace for being itself and for the knowledge of God, we are the same.

A Fuller Picture of Hospitality

The prospect of changing existing worship practices or creating new forms of outreach to be hospitable to intellectually disabled people and their families may seem daunting. Indeed, building congregations in which intellectually disabled people not only are present but are beloved friends, contributors to ministry, and partners in serving the world will take work. The good news is that it will take the sort of work of welcoming the stranger that the church at its fullest has long sought to perform, and it will make the church a more gift-filled community. Stories of discrimination currently are widespread, but stories of hope are emerging too as communities grow in hospitality. My friend Victoria has found a church home in which to share her gifts and will soon become a member. Communities that are moving toward fuller inclusion—and the people they are newly including—can provide further hope and practical guidance for other congregations.

As prior efforts to embrace marginalized peoples have helped equip churches for the now-pressing work of welcoming intellectually disabled people and their families, the church may see with fresh eyes who yet remains excluded and begin to welcome them too. Ultimately, the church can take comfort in the knowledge that it is God who unites us as the body of Christ. This belief does not relieve the church from the responsibility to strive for full inclusion of all people, including disabled people, in its life and ministry. Rather, it affirms that Christians are called to work for the manifestation of the unity that God already has enacted, the fullness of hospitality that is God's gift to the entire human community.

DISCUSSION QUESTIONS

1. What are some potential benefits of inviting an intellectually disabled person to attend your church? What are some potential challenges?

2. If your congregation currently includes intellectually disabled people, how are you supporting them and their families or caregivers during church programs and beyond?

3. If you or someone in your family is intellectually disabled, what do you think your church does well in providing hospitality? What would you like to see it do differently?

4. Do you imagine that God relates differently to intellectually disabled people than to nondisabled people? Do you imagine that intellectually disabled people relate differently to God than nondisabled people do? Why or why not?

5. Does contemplating the role of intellectually disabled people in your congregation—whether they are absent, present but not engaged in ministry, or among those who are visible leaders of the community—help you see that anyone else is missing? Who?

NOTES

1. Many churches also contain obstacles—both physical and ideological—to the participation of physically disabled people. For example, stairs and narrow hallways may prevent people who use wheelchairs from entering the building or sanctuary, and the absence of Braille worship bulletins or Bible readings may limit the participation of people who are blind or visually impaired. Further, discriminatory attitudes about what it means to be "able-bodied" may discourage nondisabled churchgoers from welcoming and accepting the gifts of physically disabled people. While physically and intellectually disabled people are excluded in ways that are sometimes meaningfully different, negative attitudes about disability are a common problem. Churches and theologians have devoted less attention to intellectual than to physical disability, though there are growing efforts to seek the inclusion of intellectually disabled people. For a groundbreaking discussion of theology and physical disability, see Nancy L. Eiesland, *The Disabled God: Toward a Liberatory Theology of Disability* (Nashville: Abingdon, 1994).

2. Brett Webb-Mitchell, *Dancing with Disabilities: Opening the Church to All God's Children* (Cleveland: United Church Press, 1994), 4.

3. For thorough discussions of God's creative relating to humanity and of human value and dignity, see David Kelsey, *Eccentric Existence: A Theological Anthropology* (Louisville: Westminster John Knox, 2009); and Kathryn Tanner, *The Politics of God: Christian Theologies and Social Justice* (Minneapolis: Fortress, 1992).

4. World Council of Churches, "Baptism, Eucharist and Ministry" (Geneva, 1982), 20.

5. Tara, October 26, 2011 (7:00 a.m.), comment on Amanda Broadfoot, "Church with the Special Needs Child," *Life Is a Spectrum Blog*, March 21, 2010, http://www.lifeisaspectrum.com/Church-with-the-special-needs-child.

6. Brett Webb-Mitchell calls this phenomenon of offering separate services the creation of faith community ghettos for disabled people. See Brett Webb-Mitchell, *Beyond Accessibility: Toward Full Inclusion of People with Disabilities in Faith Communities* (New York: Church Publishing, 2010), 80–81.

7. Quoted in Broadfoot, "Church with the Special Needs Child."

CHAPTER 9

How Should I Pray?

LGBTQ Youth Ministry in Black Church Traditions

JENNIFER S. LEATH

Learning to Pray

"May I pray with you, Kidd?" I said. "Sure. Thanks, Pastor," replied Kidd. I hesitated a moment and then began to pray. "Kidd" and "crisis" had almost become synonymous. Kidd had grown up in the church I was assigned to pastor but had never lived in one household for more than a couple years. Kidd's mother had contracted HIV before Kidd was born and had died of complications associated with AIDS by the time Kidd was three years old.

Kidd was named "Mercedes" at birth and raised primarily by her maternal grandmother. In fact, even into Kidd's early twenties Kidd did not know that grandmother was not "mother." From the age of five, Kidd was prescribed antipsychotic drugs for behavior regulation. Because of the nature of Kidd's emotional/behavioral disturbance, this meant that, in various ways, Kidd was separated from the general student population throughout primary and secondary school. By the age of twenty-five, Kidd had given birth to a son, Elijah, and had attempted suicide. Now Kidd struggles to stay sober while finding and maintaining adequate food, shelter, and employment.

For people living in crossroads of crises like Kidd's, fellowship and worship in some black congregations can be uncomfortable. In response to generations of racism in society, such congregations have built an ethos of social uplift through class mobility, color consciousness, educational aspiration, and patriarchal and heterosexual gender/sexual norms.[1] Other congregations—with varying degrees of success, and often out of necessity, open their doors to a certain degree, reluctantly tolerating the presence of young adults such as Kidd, or proactively developing ministries that positively and responsively support young adults like Kidd.

In the small African Methodist Episcopal (AME) church I pastor, Kidd is a relative of most of the twenty-five people who come to church on a regular basis. On one hand, Kidd's relatives are no longer able to support Kidd because of the extent and persistence of Kidd's mental illness, emotional instability, and inability or unwillingness to resist temptations of substance abuse, illegal means of making money, and dishonesty. On the other hand, Kidd's relatives love Kidd and want Kidd to experience the love and support of a community. Kidd's presence at church evokes ambivalence, fear, shame, and discomfort, as well as hope in the possibility of transformation. The church—for Kidd and Kidd's family—becomes a mediating space. Within this mediating space prayer is distinguished as a unifying common denominator: Kidd prays, Kidd's family prays, I pray, and the church prays.

Lessons in Prayer

No single issue is an adequate focus of prayer for Kidd, Kidd's family, or the church family of which Kidd is a part. Kidd was born into crises affected by race, class, gender, and sexuality. Sometimes Kidd and Kidd's family have weathered these crises well. However, as Kidd flounders in search of stability, these crises—some of which Kidd creates and perpetuates—wear on Kidd and Kidd's family. Together we stand in the need of prayer. What is it to pray with and for Kidd, Kidd's family, and the church of which Kidd is a member?

In Matthew 6, Jesus offers us two of his several lessons in prayer: (1) "Whenever you pray, do not be like the hypocrites; for they love to stand and pray in the synagogues and at the street corners, so that they may be seen by others. Truly I tell you, they have received their reward"; and (2) "When you are praying, do not heap up empty phrases as the Gentiles do; for they think that they will be heard because of their many words" (Matthew 6:5,7). In this passage, Jesus reminds us that prayer is not for casting impressive, respectable appearances, but for a genuine, authentic communication with G*d.[2] Prayer demands unequivocal honesty. Through prayer, we submit ourselves before G*d.

In contrast, prayer as a public demonstration of self-righteousness—especially in the midst of community crises exacerbated by class, race, gender, and sexuality—is hypocrisy. Such public prayer is rarely accompanied by private supplications, earnest dependence on G*d, and practical work toward social empowerment for "the least" among us. Prayer as a public demonstration denies the seriousness of social challenges and G*d's true power to change those circumstances. Empty phrases, many words, and vain repetitions also miss the point of prayer: G*d already knows what we need. Realism, timeliness, and relevance are essential for "good" prayer. The challenge of prayer is to guard our hearts and minds, souls and bodies such that our prayers are prayed for Divine audience.

What does all this mean in Kidd's case? We acknowledge G*d's wisdom, power, and goodness while we, like Job, declare our concern:

> I cry to you and you do not answer me; I stand, and you merely look at me. You have turned cruel to me; with the might of your hand you persecute me. You lift me up on the wind, you make me ride on it, and you toss me about in the roar of the storm. I know that you will bring me to death, and to the house appointed for all living. Surely one does not turn against the needy, when in disaster they cry for help. Did I not weep for those whose day was hard? Was not my soul grieved for the poor? But when I looked for good, evil came; and when I waited for light, darkness came. (Job 30:20-26)

With the likes of Job, we strive toward humble righteousness and pray G*d's mercy for the times we did *not* weep for those whose day was hard. Thus, when we ask, "May I pray with you, Kidd?" this request comes with a commitment to yielding our mind to the mind of Christ, standing in Job's posture, and stepping into Kidd's shoes.

We could pray:

> *Dear G*d, You alone are holy. Our crises overwhelm us, those crises that have met us on the journey and those crises we have created; we need your help. We have tried, but often failed to care for others who need your help; have mercy on us. May your Holiness deliver us from the many crises and trials we face and transform us into ambassadors of your grace, mercy, and peace—even when we wait long for your help.*

Yet a generalized prayer such as this one does not answer the real, relevant, and urgent necessity for intercession. So, instead, when I prayed with Kidd on one particular day, I focused on the specific circumstances Kidd was facing. However, my prayer seemed to fall short—not for lack of attention to the circumstances; rather, my words felt increasingly ineffective, as if they were getting caught like snagged clothing on the personal pronouns. With every phrase it became clearer that common prayer requires a delicate balance between attending singularly to divine audience and authentically reflecting the sanctified hearts and minds, bodies and souls of those gathered in prayer.

A Both/And Gender and Sexuality

To many observers, based on clothing choices and haircut, Kidd looks like a young black man. However, Kidd's physique reflects a different biological identity, and knowledge of Kidd's bearing a son seems to confirm that Kidd is anatomically female. When Kidd comes to church, Kidd is "Mercedes" to everyone. (Kidd is related to most of the church members.) However, on one occasion Kidd spoke about "other brothers," friends among whom

Kidd identifies. So I asked: "Mercedes, by what name do you prefer to be called?"

Kidd answered, "My brothers call me M-Money . . . or Kidd. You can just call me Kidd, Pastor."

Still, I didn't fully understand. So I asked a follow-up question: "Should I call you 'Kidd' at church?"

Kidd replied, "No, at church Mercedes is cool. Everybody there knows me like that—and with Elijah . . . I don't want him to ever be confused about who his mother is. I'm his mother. . . . But, yeah, when we're just talkin', you can call me 'Kidd.'"

Even still, when we prayed, I got confused. Repetitions of "Kidd" switched to "she" and "her." After praying in this way, I said: "Kidd, I am really sorry, but I need you to help me with something. How should I pray for you? Would you prefer that I refer to you as 'she' or 'he'? When *you* pray, how do you understand yourself before G*d? Who are you to G*d with respect to these categories? Who do you believe G*d understands *you* to be with respect to these categories? I ask because I want to pray *with* you, as you would pray, in the way that you understand yourself and G*d to be. I want to honor you and your physical integrity in the ways I acknowledge *you* and *your* need before G*d."

Kidd gently replied, "He. 'He' is cool." The challenge of expressing Kidd's gender identity was not a matter of articulating a fixed transgender identity. The challenge of expressing Kidd's gender identity was its everyday, practical, socially mediated fluidity. The challenge of expressing Kidd's gender identity was also the fact that, in the same instance, a masculine gender pronoun and a feminine gender pronoun could cause offense—if spoken in a pejorative tone or in a spirit of judgment.

Every day, Kidd code switches with respect to his/her gender identity. The church context through which I have encountered Kidd amplifies this fluidity—be it chosen under duress, chosen according to Kidd's most comfortable experiences of reality, and/or a natural expression of who G*d has created and is creating Kidd to be. In church Kidd is "Mercedes," yet before G*d in prayer "Mercedes" is Kidd—that is, him or he. Still, even this classification and these rules are imperfect. With respect to the biological question of sex, Kidd is a woman, and with respect to the social question of gender, Kidd is male *and* female. With respect to matters of gender and sex, Kidd calls those who would pray with him into a more nuanced, fluid, and conscious approach.

Who Do You Say That I Am?

The challenge Kidd presents to our church and other Christian communities extends beyond gender and sex. Kidd presses us to contemplate sexuality both with *and* beyond easily or permanently fixed identity categories such as "gay," "lesbian," "bisexual," or even "transgender." Kidd speaks of his "baby daddy," his "baby mama," and his female "fiancée." In different ways, Kidd reveals that he has been sexually intimate with individuals gendered as male and female, and Kidd explains his excitement that marriage between two women will be legal one day soon— so that he can marry the woman he calls his fiancée. Ultimately, Kidd expresses a sexuality that is not easily explained in biological or sociological terms. Kidd forces these questions: What *are* holy parameters for sexual identity and expression? And *how* are such parameters discerned, established, and maintained? Beyond a gender/sex identity reference, how should I pray with respect to varied expressions of sexuality?

On the one hand, with respect to Kidd's gender/sex expression, we might be tempted to quote Deuteronomy 22:5 ("A woman shall not wear a man's apparel, nor shall a man put on a woman's garment; for whoever does such things is abhorrent to the LORD your God"). Or, with respect to Kidd's sexual expressions of same-gender desire, we might be tempted to quote Romans 1:26 ("For this reason God gave them up to degrading passions. Their women exchanged natural intercourse for unnatural"). On the other hand, we might be inclined to remember the specific context out of which biblical gender/sex/sexuality mores were articulated. Further, we might hold all mores under the chief commandment of love (John 13:34: "I give you a new commandment, that you love one another. Just as I have loved you, you also should love one another"), refocusing on the fuller implications of sacred words such as these: "There is no longer Jew or Greek, there is no longer slave or free, there is no longer male and female; for all of you are one in Christ Jesus" (Galatians 3:28).

And what would this 185-year-old community of believers of which Kidd is a part be if they—having been initially composed of runaway and freed slaves—had chosen to emphasize the words "Slaves, obey your earthly masters in everything, not only while being watched and in order to please them, but wholeheartedly, fearing the Lord" (Colossians 3:22)? Somehow, in these circumstances, a way of faith and faithfulness to G*d was discerned and practiced—a g*dly standard that refused to compromise human dignity and integrity.

Biblical proof texting is insufficient for the task of discerning g*dly standards for sex and sexuality. Moreover, submitting to the patriarchal and heterosexist norms that framed the vast majority of Christian texts is inadequate for this task of discernment today. Womanist theologian Marcia Riggs, expanding on the work of feminist Christine Gudorf, writes that as members of the Christian church, we are called (or "pushed") to address these considerations:

> 1. Accepting responsibility for constructing a sexual ethic for humans rather than displacing responsibility for human codes onto God. 2. Recognizing that what Christian faith and tradition contribute to the construction of a sexual ethic is not specific sexual rules, but the concept of behavioral limits based in concern for the dignity and welfare of all persons, for justice between groups, and for love of neighbor and the common good.[3]

The specificity of behavioral limits—and their enforcement—must, then, at times give way to grander appeals to a way of individual and community faithfulness (see John 8:1-11). Alongside Scripture and tradition, and in line with John Wesley's quadrilateral approach, reason and experience are worthy factors to be considered in the work of discerning a g*dly way with respect to sex and sexuality. It is through the concepts of reason and experience that we are reminded of our subjectivities *even* as Christian believers. In other words, no two disciples of Jesus share the exact same experience of Christ. No two disciples of Jesus reason in the exact same way, coming to knowledge of Christ by identical processes.

A Faithful Response to G*d's Love

In many ways, Kidd's reality is different from my own. I do not struggle to identify my sex as female or my gender as a woman. Most of the time, I express these aspects of my identity in ways that are obvious to the communities to which I belong. While I do feel same-gender sexual attraction—and sometimes opposite-gender sexual attraction too—I know (for myself) that a holy standard and covenant with G*d and others call me toward sexual intimacy expressed in committed, monogamous relationship. The fluidity that characterizes so much of Kidd's experience of sex and sexuality are foreign to me.

The most specific sexual standard I might present to Kidd is one that builds on these key questions: What are the most complete ways that *you* can express your love for G*d—with all of your heart, mind, and soul—through your expressions of sex and sexuality? What are the most complete ways that *you* can express your love for other people—in ways that reflect G*d's equal love for you and other people—through your expressions of sex and sexuality? What are the most complete ways that *you* can express your love for *yourself*—in ways that reflect G*d's love for you—through your expressions of sex and sexuality? When your understanding of love is best aligned with G*d's perfect love, and when you answer these questions altogether, what is *your* faithful response through sex and sexuality?

Although I can present Kidd with what Scripture, tradition, reason, and experience teach me with respect to sex and sexuality, true discipleship requires that Kidd realize for himself the fullest implications of Scripture, tradition, reason, and experience.

Walking in the way of Jesus requires that Kidd apply the truth of which his heart and mind, body and soul are convicted. Surely the measures of discipleship cannot demand more than the peace of a convicted soul—formed in relationship with G*d, committed to accountability within community, and striving to dissolve the burdens that oppress the weak.

On the one hand, we might (finally) have to acknowledge that our expressions of sexuality—that complex component of human identity that encompasses "an individual's sex, gender identity and expression, and sexual orientation"[4]—and even our success in abiding by the standards we accept—have little to do with the matter of how we pray. This is especially the case when we pray independently, in our "prayer closets." In fact, in such individual prayer, the gender pronouns that paralyzed my prayer with Kidd are irrelevant. When we commune with G*d in prayer as individuals, we rarely pray with an immediate consciousness of our sexuality unless we are praying *about* some aspect of our sexuality. On the other hand, when we join together in communal prayer, the English language often *demands* a response with respect to sex (for example, gender specific pronouns), often implicating gender identity and sexual orientation. For the dignity and integrity of the individuals and communities with whom we pray, gender pronouns often mean a great deal.

Inasmuch as communal prayer calls us into both humility and authenticity—into both an acknowledgment of the divine audience and care for the integrity of community and the individuals who compose it, I felt a holy obligation to ask Kidd, "How should I pray for you?" I am convicted of a holy obligation to pray *with* Kidd *where* Kidd is with respect to sexuality. The complexity of Kidd's experiences of sexuality is no justification for refusing a dignified consciousness of sexuality—even in prayer—that affirms Kidd's humanity and the sacredness of Kidd's life *as* Kidd understands his life. Where Kidd is—living in a both/and crossroads of gender identity and sexual orientation—cannot be subjected to the confusions, misunderstandings, and prejudices of those of us who don't live there.

Crisis Management

Beyond the complex factors of sexuality, experiences of oppression, discrimination, and rejection point to the need for justice to be done with respect to LGBTQ people and communities—and especially black youth among these LGBTQ people and communities. For those of us with heteronormative commitments regarding sex and sexuality, it can be hard to *imagine* praying with Kidd *as* Kidd is—without focusing on changing Kidd's sexuality, much less doing ministry with, to, and for LGBTQ people like Kidd.

There are many of us within black church traditions who are unable to address any other crisis young adults like Kidd face because we are blinded by the appearance of a sexuality that deviates from our sense of "normal." Sociologist Cathy Cohen notes, "Black youth who are more religious are 13 percent *more likely* than the least religious black youth to agree" that "it is always wrong to have sex before you are married," "homosexuality is always wrong," and "abortion is always wrong."[5] At the same time, the contemporary emphasis of LGBTQ rights movements has been on marriage equality.

In a report of the Center for American Progress, "Jumping beyond the Broom: Why Black Gay and Transgender Americans Need More than Marriage Equality," Aisha C. Moodie-Mills explains the unique hardships of "economic insecurity," "low educational attainment," and "health and wellness disparities" that black LGBTQ individuals face. Arguing that, ultimately, black LGBTQ individuals and communities stand in need of a defense of rights *other* than marriage, Moodie-Mills writes, "Whereas one in five transgender Americans are denied a home or apartment on the basis of their gender identity that figure doubles to two in five for black transgender Americans."[6] In other words, a variety of challenges face black queer youth—many of which are exacerbated by gender identity and sexual orientation. Although Kidd is excited about the possibility of marriage, Kidd's everyday concern is *literally* where he will live.

When those of us within black churches and communities decide to ignore, avoid, or otherwise discriminate against people in Kidd's position, we are not upholding a righteous banner of respectability; we are not defending a holy standard of sexual purity. When we in black churches and communities make life harder on people like Kidd, we are ceding our righteousness. We are refusing care for orphans; we are refusing homes for those without shelter; we are refusing food to those who are hungry; we are refusing clothing to those who are inadequately clothed; and we are refusing love to those who feel unloved. In fact, we are *creating* and exacerbating the very conditions to which Christ calls us to minister (see Matthew 25).

Kidd—and all those who live in the crossroads of intersecting forms of oppression—stands in need of more creative approaches to *both* prayer *and* practical forms of crisis management that extend from prayer. Kidd demands crisis management that *at least* focuses on alleviating the disproportionate socioeconomic injustices Kidd faces—even if an acceptance of Kidd's fluid sexuality is not possible.

Quiet Movements and Terms of Engagement

Emilie Townes has helpfully challenged the preoccupation with homophobia in black churches and communities. She explains that prior to the demand that identity politics placed on individuals and communities to name (and continually rename) themselves with respect to sexuality, diverse expressions were part of the social fabric of black churches and communities. Though unnamed, she contends, these diverse expressions of sexuality were not necessarily targets of discrimination.[7]

While Townes may be correct about that historic lack of discrimination, it is dangerous to return to (or persist in) ignoring or maintaining "respectful" silence around the diversities of sexuality within black churches and communities—particularly in light of the broad social needs that such diversities imply. Equally dangerous, however, is for black churches and communities to cede the terms of engagement with respect to sexuality to the voices and interests of the dominant culture in the United States (that is, allowing dominant culture to dictate the labels and meanings associated with sexual discourse). We must take great care to avoid both of these dangers. Although sexuality should be addressed directly, it is not necessary that sexuality be named in the ways that have become most entrenched in US culture.

The question of how to discuss matters of human sexuality in black church contexts is not simply a practical matter of how to lovingly and respectfully respond to diverse expressions of identity. In a postmodern society, even when it appears that identity does not matter, it does. Between the two extremes within the economy of closeting identity of "don't ask, don't tell" and "identity doesn't matter, so we don't have to name ourselves," the lives of children of God are at stake.

Kidd demands that a movement, heretofore quiet, take up new terms of engagement, birthing and renewing deep commitments to justice. Kidd demands a common language of prayerful praxis for people "in the life"—for whom race and poverty are factors of equal significance to that of sexuality. Kidd demands a common language of prayerful praxis that addresses the differences between sex and gender. Kidd demands a common language of prayerful praxis that addresses the diverse ways that sexuality is expressed. How, then, will we pray?

DISCUSSION QUESTIONS

1. How does our intercessory prayer for others acknowledge the sacred value, integrity, and dignity of those for whom we pray?

2. How do we identify, prioritize, and approach social crises within our communities?

3. How do we respond to intersecting forms of oppression— and intersecting forms of identity in ways that disrupt both structural/systemic and interpersonal evils?

4. Does your church minister to queer individuals and communities? How?

5. How do you pray for and with those who are most different from you?

NOTES

1. Evelyn Brooks Higginbotham, *Righteous Discontent: The Women's Movement in the Black Baptist Church, 1880–1920* (Cambridge: Harvard University Press, 1993).

2. Elisabeth Schüssler Fiorenza explains her use of the notion "G*d" in reference to the Divine Source. She writes: "In order to indicate the brokenness and inadequacy of human language to name the Divine, I switched in my book *Jesus: Miriam's Child, Sophia's Prophet; Critical Issues in Feminist Christology* (New York: Continuum, 1994) from the Orthodox Jewish writing of *G-d*, which I had adopted in *But She Said: Feminist Practices of Biblical Interpretation* (Boston: Beacon, 1992) and *Discipleship of Equals: A Critical Feminist Ekklēsia-logy of Liberation* (New York: Crossroad, 1993), to the spelling *G*d*, which seeks to avoid the conservative malestream association that the writing of *G-d* has for some Jewish feminists. Consequently, I have begun to write also *the*logy*, which literally means 'speaking of G*d,' in the same way in order to indicate that I speak about G*d neither in masculine (*theology*) nor in feminine (*thealogy*) gender terms." I have adopted this denotation for divinity, sharing in this rationale. Elisabeth Schüssler Fiorenza, "Feminist Studies in Religion and The*logy: In-Between Nationalism and Globalism: Roundtable Lead-In," accessed October 8, 2013, http://www.fsrinc.org/article/624.

3. Marcia Riggs, *Plenty Good Room: Women Versus Male Power in the Black Church* (Cleveland, OH: Pilgrim, 2003), 27.

4. Definition of sexuality (as an area of study) taken from the website of the American Psychological Association (APA), accessed October 7, 2013, http://www.apa.org/topics/search.aspx?query=sexuality.

5. Cathy J. Cohen, *Democracy Remixed: Black Youth and the Future of American Politics*, Kindle ed. (New York: Oxford University Press, 2010), 64.

6. Aisha C. Moodie-Mills, *Jumping beyond the Broom: Why Black Gay and Transgender Americans Need More Than Marriage Equality* (Center for American Progress, 2012), 18.

7. Emilie M. Townes, "The Dancing Mind: Queer Black Bodies and Activism in Academy and Church: 2011 Gilberto Castañeda Lecture" (Chicago Theological Seminary, Chicago, October 28, 2011).

CHAPTER 10

Listening for God in Community

Relationships of Christian Transformation

ALISON VANBUSKIRK PHILIP

Experiencing God's Presence in Christian Community

Growing up outside of the church, I thought Christianity was about judgment, fear, and dividing the world into "us" and "them." In college, when many of my friends were drifting away from the church, I was drawn in—first cautiously and then wholeheartedly. The church that I found (and that also found me) offered a dynamic experience of listening in community and experiencing God's presence. This encounter with Christianity unmistakably reconfigured my earlier impressions. In the grace of discovering Christian community, it became clearer to me that faith is rooted in relationship first to God and then to one another.

From this perspective of relationship, I read the Bible in its entirety for the first time and began to see that it is God's story, to which we are invited to join our stories as God shapes us and our lives. I experienced church as a community of people who together seek to listen to God and one another through Scripture, prayer, and fellowship. This community is the body of Christ that serves and proclaims the gospel—not as fear-inducing news, but as truly good, life-transforming, world-altering news that can impact not only individuals but all of creation.

After college I had the opportunity to work for four years with a global women's movement called World Day of Prayer. It solidified my understanding of what church can be and what it needs to be more of the time as it plays its part in proclaiming and ushering in God's kingdom among us. Engaging with women from around the world and participating in their prayer services reinforced my belief that listening and community are deeply needed in our globalizing world. These experiences offered in me a vision of Christianity that flows as a life-giving stream within local communities and among different perspectives, cultures, and generations.

Meanwhile I became more and more involved in my local congregation, where I participate in a covenant group of young adults who gather to support one another in our faith. As a group, we share our walks with God, and we walk together through life changes: new relationships, new jobs, weddings, pregnancies, deaths. Our time together is a space for being vulnerable and honest, admitting all for which we do not have answers in our lives and in our faith. It is a space for listening instead of always speaking and for recognizing how we all need to be heard. We have learned and relearned that God gives us the gift of one another and that God is palpably present among us "where two or three are gathered in [Christ's] name" (Matthew 18:20).

Listening in Community

My experience of God at work in individual lives and communities starts with listening in community. While God's action takes place at the big-picture level, it also takes place at the level of particulars. The question "What is God doing in the world?" is also a question of "What is God doing in my community? What is God doing in my life?" God's particularity in the Incarnation is echoed in the way God comes now into our particular contexts. We live fully into our particulars through faith in God who knows the whole picture, a picture we can only glimpse as through a mirror, dimly (1 Corinthians 13:12).

The contexts where I have experienced listening for God in the details have revealed to me what church can be: prayerful community where Christ is at work forgiving, transforming, and creating space for individuals to hear God's voice in their lives and in the life of the world. World Day of Prayer as a local yet global movement has taught me how each local community listening for God and listening to each other impacts the wider community and world. My covenant group has offered me a particular form and experience of this kind of community of listening and prayer that has ancient roots in the early church, that persisted in monastic movements and through the Reformation, and that moves us forward as the church into God's future. Both of these communities invite us into our role as partners in God's work in the world by opening spaces for connection to God and other people.

In prayer, God listens to us—regardless of gender, age, race, denomination, education level, or socioeconomic situation. We in turn are invited to listen to one another and to one another's prayers. In individual and collective prayers, such as those prayed on World Day of Prayer and in covenant group, God's Spirit is present with us and with our sisters and brothers nearby and across the globe. This Spirit invites us to be honest with one another about the realities of our experience. Honesty enables us to have true dialogue, sharing, and authentic human connection. We see God at work in one another and ourselves, and we are enlarged and emboldened for the work of love in our world. Solidarity becomes more possible as prayer paves a path for united movement. How we move and exist in the world aligns with what we together have learned and shared. The body parts realize that they are connected, that they rely on one another, and that the body benefits when the parts act together (1 Corinthians 12).

Thus, we can no longer live in the same way after hearing the voices of our sisters and brothers, experiencing their pains with them, and feeling their hopes and fears. Prayer and action are not two different things connected by a string but are inseparable realms of our faith experience. To pray is to be truly changed. To act in accordance with these changes happens organically; our prayer continues in action. We perceive, receive, and point to God's work among us with our words, deeds, and very being.

Hearing Us into Speech

To hear a group of people into speaking means to invite them to share truthfully from the depths of their social, political, economic, psychological, and spiritual location.[1] Jesus' ministry was one of hearing as well as teaching and healing. It was in part through being receptive to the people around him that Jesus served, taught, and healed them. As Christ's body, the church inherits a role of listening as well as a role of proclaiming. Providing an open and receptive ear creates space for others to join in the conversation, to be known as part of the community, and to find their voices in connection to God. I witnessed how this can happen at the global level through the ecumenical women's movement, World Day of Prayer.

The World Day of Prayer (WDP) movement offers an example of how the church can move forward as one body in a global, multifaith world. World Day of Prayer is an ecumenical movement of Christian women that has its roots in the late nineteenth century. On the first Friday of March, World Day of Prayer begins when the sun rises in Tonga and continues until it sets in Samoa. During that time tens of thousands of local communities in more than 170 countries participate in a common ecumenical worship service focused on a biblical theme that is prepared by women of a different country each year and translated into more than a hundred languages worldwide. This liturgy of prayer and worship is woven from women's stories and experiences that shape and are shaped by their faith. Through this liturgy and the photos, historical information, art, and music that go with it, WDP listens to women's voices, cultivates genuine dialogue and honest sharing among diverse people, and encourages action that promotes justice and healing. It works for unity and peace by linking one individual to another, one culture to another, in an ever-expanding circle in which we are held together in Christ as we continually seek to welcome in others.

World Day of Prayer emphasizes that authentic community is the circle where this profound listening takes place, where change originates, healing unfolds, and peace grows. The movement stresses that we each live and breathe in our local community. Together these many communities make up our global community, our global movement of prayer. We find this emphasis on community in the Gospels as well as in early Christian history. The Greek word for ecumenism means the "inhabited world" and has its root in the concept of "house." We are rooted in God's great household, where we live and grow together as the body of Christ.

World Day of Prayer is rooted in the realization that we are already part of God's household, the body of Christ in the world.[2] We pray and grow in our relationship with God, and doing so prepares us to relate to people around us and around the world in a receptive way. This is our peace-building, kingdom-building work. It is work that recognizes our unity in Christ within our diverse cultures, life experiences, and church traditions. It values how we are similar as well as the many ways in which we are different. We are a tapestry of vibrantly colored threads woven together into one fabric through our prayer to God.

With this understanding in mind, each local WDP committee works to make its community a safe place for women to speak. This safe place grounds the women in the truth of who they are and what they experience. It also strengthens them to move forward from that location in collective action. When women are grounded and empowered to speak their voice(s), they find strength to build more peaceful realities for themselves and their children.[3] When women listen to the voices of other women, they are also encouraged to participate in creative action with their sisters, both locally and globally.[4] Thus, we build peace through prayer that unfolds into action at the grassroots level within communities as well as across communities, continents, and oceans.

In prayerful listening, both the speaker and hearer are receptive to God's presence moving among and between them. By speaking their voice and owning their story, the women of the writer country gain courage and confidence to stand up for justice and to move forward in hope and faith. As they find themselves in prayer and hear the power in their stories, they know what their work in the world is and discover their strength. By being heard through their prayers, they feel encouraged to claim who they are and to act in accordance with the eternal realities of faith, hope, and love toward which their prayers point.

A powerful instance of this kind of prayer comes from the women of Papua New Guinea. Throughout decades of celebrating worship services from other countries, they faithfully listened to their sisters. When they wrote the service in 2009, they were eager to tell their stories to women around the world. They offered examples of women who fought for peace during a time of civil war and violence in their country. They shared about the suffering that Papua New Guineans face as a result of environmental destruction and rampant HIV and AIDS. Following the celebration of WDP in 2009, the women reflected on their experience:

> Perhaps the most powerful part of being a writer country was the opportunity for us to tell our stories. Through the narration of our lives, we learned that we do not have to be afraid or ashamed of standing up for and speaking about our rights. WDP has given us confidence and trust in God to speak up for truth and to empower one another. Being able to share our experiences with women around the globe filled us up with even more courage and strength, encouraging us to move forward with our work for peace.[5]

World Day of Prayer provided an opportunity for the women of Papua New Guinea to share from their hearts, from their triumphs, and from their suffering. Doing so reinforced their sense of ownership of their lives and fostered their confidence in their ability to make a difference in their society. Faith community has this power. It is rooted in a deep receptivity to God and awareness of our dependence on God from which true personal power and agency flow. God offers God's grace and love, and we can respond in ways that reflect that grace and love into our communities.

The church as a whole can learn from WDP's emphasis on creating space for people to speak and grow in their relationships to God and one another. In an era marked by polarization, this emphasis can serve to remind the church that humanity's interconnection runs far deeper than our political and even theological divides. At the same time as the women of the writer country speak about and share their reality, we who pray with and for them realize that what affects them affects us too.

Just as we are known and empowered when we are listened to by God and one another, we also know ourselves better as we listen to and get to know our sisters. We find ourselves—through both our similarities and differences—in their prayers. When we know ourselves better, we can more fully and genuinely open ourselves to God and each other.[6] Our inner experience and outer attitudes and behaviors go together. Our particular situation and the wider world around us are linked. World Day of Prayer's awareness of this interconnectedness of global community led me to pay more attention to the inner and outer dynamics of prayer in my own particular local community.

Saying How We Really Are

Since the first century, Christian community has been rooted in prayer (Acts 2:42). Prayer takes us to the rawest and most real parts of ourselves and our world. When we lift those parts to God, we can receive God's transformation and healing. Getting to that place of recognition and surrender is a challenge. It is painful and at times feels shameful to see and share what we really are. Yet without recognizing what we are, it is harder to turn to God with our whole selves to ask for God's healing mercy.

Being known by others in community requires being seen. It can feel easier to hide what we are out of fear or shame. American culture is rife with these isolating forces: we want to be successful and have ourselves together at all times. We want to be comfortable, to have all we need, to be independent. Yet when we're honest, we know that we don't have it all together. We know that we need each other. There is a pervasive longing for community in our culture of moving around, getting things done, and being individuals.

Christian community challenges our instinct to remain hidden. It challenges our culture of independence and productivity. Praying in community slows us down, asks us to really look at ourselves, and pushes us to see what keeps us separated from those around us. God's Spirit steps in and creates for us a space, not of judgment, hiding, and shame (see Genesis 3), but of mercy and grace, of receiving and sharing love. The Holy Spirit steps in and offers us another way. It points us to the reign of God at hand. Christian community is rooted in God's purpose "to share with [humankind] the life and love which he has within himself" as Trinity.[7] God invites us into the intimate fellowship that exists within God's triune being of Father, Son, and Spirit. This community of love and joy is also God's purpose and work in the world for us.

While we cannot make this kind of community on our own, we are called to prepare ourselves to receive God's gift of community and to be receptive to ways the community can move and grow. The covenant group ministry at my church in New York seeks to respond to God's movement by offering spaces of intentional community in the hustle and bustle of modern life. Groups agree (or covenant) to meet together regularly for an initial period of three or four months, to pray together, and to discuss Scripture or a spiritually focused book. Each person commits to be present, to keep confidentiality, to keep up with the reading, and to pray for the others in the group. After the initial period, people can choose to continue or to stop with no pressure. This format offers a balance of commitment and flexibility.

When I first moved to New York, I longed for the kind of genuine community that the covenant groups hope to foster. I wanted it so much that I jumped into a group that was struggling to keep going. We stuck it out through almost a year of hesitant meetings and difficult conversations before the group decided that it would be best to let go. It made me cautious to try again. Were these groups merely ideals that in reality were messy, requiring reckless vulnerability? It seemed we could not do anything to *make* God be present with us.

After a year of sitting with this question, sensing a shared longing for prayerful friendships among some peers, and feeling a spark from God to take the risk of trying something, I invited ten people attending the church to meet for five months. During those months, we had scattered attendance. Our times together of prayer, discussion, and sharing were consistent but not earthshaking. By summer a couple of people chose not to continue and a couple moved away. The rest of us decided to keep going. We met at one woman's apartment to discuss our way ahead. We spoke from our hearts. Something gently and gracefully gelled at that meeting. A new level of trust glided into the space of our group. It surprised and warmed us, and we welcomed it with open arms.

In time our prayers deepened. Instead of closing with a general prayer, we added new specificity. Our prayer requests became the most essential part of our experience. They became a time "to say how we really are," as one participant has expressed it. They became a space for us to be really honest about what is going on in our hearts and minds. That time of praying and sharing has been transformative. God has used it to open our hearts to each other and to God's work in our lives. It has illustrated for me that "no one can hear God's word or believe by themselves."[8] God gives us fellowship with one another. We are not self-reliant. We depend first on God and also on the others God places in our lives.

As a group we have grown in our faith, wrestled with hard questions, found support through exciting and painful life changes, and experienced a living sense of God's presence with and among us. We have helped each other see through the grime in our lives and selves to glimpse our truest gifts and live in more constant awareness of God's grace. Our friendships have grown not out of our own efforts but out of a soft but palpable breeze of God's goodness and care for us. We made the commitment to show up, and something greater than us swept in and made us community.

While I do not understand what causes one group to work and one not to, I think it is crucial to trust that God is at work even in the frustrations and apparent failures. As Dietrich Bonhoeffer stresses in his classic book *Life Together*, "Christian [fellowship] is not an ideal which we must realize; it is rather a reality created by God in Christ in which we may participate."[9] Bonhoeffer warns against our tendency to seek an ideal community that meets all our individual desires. The point is not what we want. The point is gratefully receiving God's gifts to us. God gives us fellowship that strengthens us as individuals and moves us beyond ourselves to caring for other people. Sometimes God's gifts are the lessons that grow out of frustration even within that fellowship. We participate in communities that are not ideal but that are where God places us, and God is at work in them.

The variety and flexibility of these covenant groups at this church alone is wide. The group that I'm part of consists of young professional women, both single and married. Other groups span generations and life experiences. Some are men's groups, some are women's groups, and some are coed. What is consistent across groups is a clear sense of what is being agreed to—a willingness to show up and be present, a commitment to pray and trust God at work, courage to face and voice frustration in respectful ways, and wisdom to ask for help when needed. In all the variety and flexibility, we exercise our faith in God's grace to us through one another. We exercise our willingness to trust, to share, and to risk vulnerability. We exercise our patience in relating to others and waiting for God. We move between the realm of God's living work in the world of the present and God's not-yet-realized reign of peace, joy, and love. We seek and we wait to find; we sow and we wait to reap. We consider how to better serve God in all aspects of our lives.

The Christian formation, commitment, and accountability that take place in these groups spills out into the life of the greater congregation. Groups often serve together in outreach activities, provide hospitality after worship services, and attend adult education classes together. They welcome new people who come to the church, and they sometimes help to form new groups. The vital depth of relationship with God and one another is not isolated to the meeting time. It shapes how we live and move and have our being in the wider community and our world. It prepares us as disciples and refines us as forgiven human beings on a journey. It helps us to really know, not just in our heads but also in our hearts and souls, that we do not walk alone.

God's Church and Our Work in the World

When I first became part of a church as a college student, I was filled with joy and wondered how I had misunderstood Christianity up until that point in my life. I was angry by the way it was represented by certain fellow Christians who used it as a political platform or mark of their personal holiness over other people; by the media who reported primarily extremes; and by people whose negative experiences had soured their opinion of all churches and all Christians. I wanted to change those impressions. I wanted to build up the church as I knew it—as a place for listening in community. I felt excited, but I also felt afraid. "Church is on the decline!" I heard all around me. What if I loved it foolishly? What if decline was unstoppable? What if I wasn't really equipped to build or change anything?

In time I recognized the naïveté of this perspective. It was colored with an alternating fear-filled and pride-filled sense of self-sufficiency, a sense that church is up to me—up to us! The church is God's church, the body of Christ, and while it may look different from the outside than in the past, it still belongs to God. It is not up to us to save the church or our place in it—God already has. In our time it seems that the church's decline is the common message around us, but decline is not the last word. God is still at work, and we are called to listen for God. What God is doing is not about restoring numbers or reviving old structures. God is ceaselessly doing a new thing and inviting us to participate. Are we listening? Are we awake?

Listening and wakening have inner and outer aspects, as World Day of Prayer and my covenant group both have illustrated for me. What God is doing within each of us is part of God's work in the world. Receiving God's kingdom within means we can speak of God's kingdom and work for God's kingdom without. God's realm is rooted in relationship. The church does not exist for itself as itself. Its existence does not depend on its relevance or popularity. Rather, the church exists for Christ as Christ's body, of which we are a part. It exists through life-giving relationship between God and us and between us and one another. These relationships connect us in a circle of community that welcomes and fosters the peace of God in individuals and groups in ways that expand outward into the world. This is the Christianity I have come to know, the church that has forever changed my life. Thanks be to God!

DISCUSSION QUESTIONS

1. In your life, when and how have you found that you connect most deeply with God? What habits and disciplines help cultivate this connection?

2. How might your church help people pray with sincerity, depth, and discipline as individuals and as a community?

3. Think of a time when someone listened to you very well and a time when someone didn't. How might you apply these experiences to how you listen to others? How does your faith impact how you listen?

4. Whose voices (individual or collective)—in your church or community—are hushed or passed over? How can you help to change this?

5. Think about a time when you have experienced authentic community. What qualities made it authentic? What are some of the ways you might help create this kind of community?

NOTES

1. Nelle Morton discusses the idea of "hearing to speech" in her book *The Journey Is Home* (Boston: Beacon, 1987), 202.

2. World Day of Prayer is rooted in a common faith in Jesus Christ, the Bible, and prayer. When speaking about our faith, we acknowledge who we are without excluding anyone else from doing the same. In our prayer and worship on WDP, we welcome those of other faiths, even as we celebrate our Christian faith in a range of styles and traditions.

3. For more perspectives on women's ability to change the world, see Nicholas Kristof and Sheryl WuDunn, *Half the Sky: Turning Oppression into Opportunity for Women Worldwide* (New York: Knopf, 2009).

4. "World Day of Prayer International Committee Guiding Principles," World Day of Prayer USA, accessed April 23, 2013, http://www.wdp-usa.org/about/.

5. World Day of Prayer Committee of Papua New Guinea, "In Christ, We Are Many Members Yet One Body," *2009 World Day of Prayer Journal* 35: 3.

6. Knowing ourselves and opening ourselves more fully is a process related to the concept of sanctification. We are justified through faith once and for all, yet God continues to work in us over the course of our lives so that we grow in our capacity for faith, hope, and love.

7. Thomas F. Torrance, *Atonement: The Person and Work of Christ*, ed. Robert T. Walker (Downers Grove, IL: InterVarsity, 2009), 359.

8. Ibid., 366.

9. Dietrich Bonhoeffer, *Life Together: The Classic Exploration of Christian Community* (New York: HarperCollins, 1954), 30.

CHAPTER 11

Eternity in the Now

The Church as Curator of Timeless Beauty

ZACHARY UGOLNIK

A Moment of Awe

The church of the future must be a church of the present. The present is the most eternal part of time, and the church must continue to offer freely an experience of eternity. By encouraging the church to be of the present, I do not mean that it should discard the traditions of the past or adapt to every trend. I am, after all, an Eastern Orthodox Christian—where the adjective *Orthodox*, meaning "right doctrine," or "right glory," is part of our name. Rather, I simply mean to point to the church's role as a conduit of grace, that mystical stuff outside of earthly time.

The more I think about what the future will look like, the more I imagine digital screens acting as mediums for how we view the world. The church, by contrast, should offer face-to-face encounters with reality and with other humans who are made in the image of God. The beauty and ritual of the church should transport us to the nontemporal aspects of the present—to that shared place between ourselves and the Divine. God is the eternal now, and we are his icons in progress, striving to realize his image through grace. The church of the future must offer experiences of this divine harmony.

As a child I always wanted to be an iconographer. At my first year at church camp in western Pennsylvania, I remember walking to the small chapel during afternoon free time. I sat in the empty pews and stared at the wooden iconostasis—the screen decorated with icons that divides the nave of the church from the altar—towering over me. The faces of the saints seemed to look into me, generating warmth in my chest similar to the feeling of being hugged by my mother or father. I prayed to God that I would become a painter of icons.

The Orthodox Church is perhaps unique in its use of visual culture. Orthodox Christians believe the incarnation of the Son of God revealed to all humanity the image of the Father. Through taking human form, the entire material world was made holy, the cosmos transfigured. Saints are thought to achieve deification in their lifetimes through the emulation of Christ, fulfilling the role of humanity as created in the image of God. Icons—which from the Greek translates as "image, likeness, or portrait"—are thus images of the images of God. The church too is called to be an image of God. And, of course, so also are we. Each of us, by calling, is an "iconographer" of our truest selves as God intended. The painted images of the saints remind us of this vocation.

The chapel's iconostasis ascended toward the ceiling in levels, portraits of saints occupying the first tier. To the left and right of the center door the Virgin Mary and Christ reigned, flanked by the archangels, John the Baptist, and other saints I didn't recognize. The next tier contained icons that depicted the major feasts of the year, including the Annunciation; the Nativity of Christ; the Crucifixion, with Mary Magdalene at Christ's side; and the Resurrection, Christ's hands reaching out to Adam and Eve in shadow. As my eyes swept up the iconostasis—a wall, a screen, an ending that is believed to represent the likeness of God—I was greeted by a crowd of holy people, as if I were seeing a mirror of humankind.

There was not an external light source, but light emanated from within the images, gold infusing all space. In contrast to famous paintings in Western art, a border did not partition the supernatural; there was not one holy section of the icon, but all was infused with Divinity. Objects and figures appeared side by side, not in their proper order related to distance and dimension, but according to their spiritual significance. Much like the family portraits I drew in childhood—family members represented by torsoless heads with protruding arms and legs—an icon attempts to capture the three-dimensional in the two dimensional, but with slightly more sophistication.

Unlike the linear perspective of the Renaissance where all space is rendered according to a unique perspective, where the lines of bodies are projected onto a plane, where the reality extends beyond the surface of the work and the eye is drawn into the horizon, Byzantine icons employ reverse perspective. Through this inversion, shapes appear in ways impossible to see from one single perspective. Instead, the image intends to demonstrate multiple perspectives. Depth is projected as if the viewer is looking from both sides of the room, a technique that influenced the Russian avant-garde painters, cubism, and, in turn, Picasso. Mountains bend backward, producing S-curves with jagged edges, evocative of movement. The back of thrones appear spherical, the right arm set apart from the curve of the left side. A bird's-eye view of the top of a table and the table's legs as they would appear from the front are visible simultaneously.

In these icons, space has no depth moving from the imagined threshold at the front of the frame toward a horizon in the back. Perspective, on the other hand, is cast outward, invading the space of the viewer. St. John of Damascus called icons "windows to heaven." However, when we gaze through them, we do not look into an abysmal void of the age to come; we see a reflection of our own world transfigured. Eternity is not found in the horizon of the picture; it is found in the world around us.

I gazed at the icons as if I were looking through all the eyes of the world. Christ and the saints look at you—teaching us to see with the compassionate eyes of the Divine. The experience of the icon teaches us that Truth (with a capital *T*) is *not* relative but is relational. Perhaps for this reason in Dostoyevsky's novel *The Idiot*, through the interaction between the characters of Ippolit and the simple Prince Myshkin, the former quoting the later, the famous phrase emerges: "Beauty will save the world."[1]

Even as a child I was able to contemplate the piety and devotion portrayed in the portraits of the saints. Looking in the painted eyes of the figures, I could sense their somber love for Christ. Icons do not attempt a realist depiction, nor do they portray the ideals of external beauty like so many Photoshopped pictures of celebrities. Icons represent the beauty within, the union achieved between the saints and Christ.

I never became an iconographer in the sense I intended. I still have some of my sketches—evidence that not all art produced is a masterpiece. But that shouldn't stop us from trying to participate in the creation of beauty, whatever the medium, to the best of our abilities. Indeed, it is perhaps the spirit of humility, sincerity, and selfless giving that most distinguishes spiritual beauty from the images that bombard our eyes in American culture.

As more individuals identify less with a particular tradition or denomination, the more responsibility churches will have to offer an experience of awe and beauty through which individuals can recognize the presence of the Divine. Beauty speaks to unbelievers in ways that are not logical, much like a picture speaking to a child. It does not argue; it simply offers an experience unselfishly. Beauty allows us to see through the eyes of our neighbor, to glimpse reality in the present moment, and to understand the divinity running through these many perspectives.

As a culture, we are continually bombarded by advertisements and images that valorize physical beauty, and this overexposure will only increase as technology advances. The church, however, must offer epiphanies of beauty that express the eternity of the Divine. This distinction is not something that needs to be explained but felt in the heart. Much of our culture is about uncovering an experience instead of simply being overwhelmed by it.

The church's duty, therefore, is to offer a sense of awe through encounters with the majesty of the Divine. The more beauty and spiritual nourishment accessible in churches, the more individuals will realize they cannot live without this grace. Beauty will allow agnostics and those who identify as "spiritual but not religious" to continually crave the experience of church and the "peace of God, which surpasses all understanding" (Philippians 4:7).

Many churches in the United States already feature local artists in their community space and hallways, host musical concerts, and consciously beautify their sanctuary and the natural assets around their buildings. Though every church may not have the budget for a three-tiered iconostasis or the arts program at the Cathedral of St. John the Divine in New York (a model program for those who do), every church can do its part in creating a community of spiritual beauty.

A Moment of Harmony

We must be vigilant, however, that the church expresses a spiritual beauty beyond time. The church must then represent equally our multiple perspectives on earth, much like the many lines of vision portrayed in painted icons. Each of us is called to be an icon of God, but inequality based on gender violates the beauty and inner harmony of the church. When a newborn child is brought to an Eastern Orthodox church for the first time, the priest welcomes the parents at the door and then carries the child down the center aisle to the altar. If the child is a girl, some priests will not walk her behind the altar (as women are traditionally not allowed behind the iconostasis without a blessing) but will instead place the child in front of the icon of the Theotokos, the mother of God or the "God-bearer," for a brief moment as they recite a prayer.

In the Greek Orthodox church I grew up in, however, the priest would always carry the child, regardless of the child's sex, through the center doors of the iconostasis and back around the altar table. As he emerged, turning toward the congregation, he would hold the child above his shoulders (in a gesture similar to the raising of Simba in *The Lion King*) and make the sign of the cross with the child, saying, "The servant of God (giving the name of the child) is churched, in the Name of the Father, and of the Son, and of the Holy Spirit. Amen."

Though I had to stop myself as a child from singing the "The Circle of Life" as I gazed at the priest in multicolored Byzantine robes holding up a newborn baby, I could not help but be overcome with the power of that moment. Here was a new baby, around forty days old, held up on this single occasion for the entire community to see, a community it would grow into and of which it would become an integral part.

When the name announced was a girl's name, I can remember my mother leaning over to me and telling me with a sense of pride, "He's not supposed to do that." Of course, in the forty years that this particular priest served the community, the parishioners came to expect the priest to always walk the child behind the altar, whether the baby's socks were pink or blue. Placing the female child in front of the icon of Theotokos is a very beautiful gesture, of course, reminding us of our role as icons of God, but it should not be used as a substitute for a blessing only accorded to male babies. As we look to the future, we must be sure the same equality my church offered that baby girl in her churching is offered throughout her life.

Too often in the Orthodox Church the veneration of the role of motherhood is held up in response to calls for gender equality and becomes an argument frequently used against the ordination of women. Men and women are not the same, the argument goes, but have equally important yet different roles: only a man can be a priest; only a woman can be a mother. It is very true that the Theotokos in the Orthodox Church has a very special role, to say the least, as we frequently sing she is "more honorable than the Cherubim, and more glorious beyond compare than the Seraphim." However, men are called to emulate the Theotokos as bearers of the Divine just as much as women; women, in turn, of course, are called to emulate Christ. Even if we do have different roles as men and women in our current society, each of us transcends those roles in our encounter with God. The ability to birth a child, though endowed with spiritual significance, is a biological distinction, of which men and women have many. We have different roles, but we each reflect the image of God.

The office of priesthood, however, is not based on biology. For this reason, the holy fathers and mothers of the church do not clearly articulate an adequate reason for why a priest must be male: for in Christ "there is no longer male and female" (Galatians 3:28). We do not revere Christ because he was a man; we revere and worship him because he is God. Christ has two natures according to Eastern Orthodox doctrine, as both God and human. The office of the priest, as conveyer of the holy sacraments that communicate the Divine into a human realm, represents that divine nature. A female, just as much as a male, can represent that office and its mystery, as each of us can equally receive the grace of the Holy Spirit. Our image of God as beyond human understanding will not change.

The main argument given against the ordination of women priests is that it was not done in the past and therefore contradicts the church's preservation of holy tradition, and with that, the grace of God. Now is not the occasion to provide a full discussion of the canons cited in debates about the ordination of women, but let me briefly suggest that tradition is not about the rote repetition of the past, but rather, in many ways, it is about the intersection of eternity into the realm of time. The church exists in an institutional reality on earth and also channels the eternal reality of the Divine. We do a disservice to the church, however, when we do not distinguish the two. When we reenact a liturgy written in the fourth century, we enable ourselves to step outside of time and to mysteriously encounter the kingdom of God on earth in the here and now. Liturgy symbolizes this intermingling.

However, the reservation of the priesthood to males does not reflect the liturgy's eternal aspect but rather the historical context in which the liturgy was developed. We have the principles of our theology to teach us this. Women were deacons in the early church, and the ordination of women to priesthood would not compromise the sanctity and timelessness of the liturgy. In my opinion, it would reinforce it. In eternity we are not distinguished by gender, wealth, or class but are seen as equal in the eyes of God. The church needs to encourage occasions where we experience this shared humanity.

Another argument along the same terms is that the ordination of women violates natural order and denigrates the church's social icon of a traditional family in which the man is always the superior. But this conception of natural order is outdated, as it was informed by the opinions of the past, not the Truth of the church. This social ideal, still advocated by many churches, no longer expresses the best of our present society. The church of the future must narrow this gap, or it risks not being able to communicate the God of the eternal now.

In my experience, the arguments given to justify the practice of not ordaining women require more summersaults of rationality than the arguments *for* women's ordination, which rely on the theological mystery of immanence and transcendence. Practice is the only precedent for not ordaining women. The justification for opposing women's ordination is not found in our theology. We demonstrate a lack of trust in the sanctity of the church and the Holy Spirit if we fear that the alteration of one practice will damage the entirety of the church.

Change, of course, in the Eastern Orthodox Church takes time. In 2004 the Holy Synod of the church of Greece restored the women's deaconate. Other Orthodox churches feel the women's deaconate does not need to be restored because it was never abolished. However, as a church community, we need to shorten the distance between policy and reality. We need to encourage girls to be acolytes; we need to encourage these same girls to pursue vocations as deacons. There is nothing stopping us from doing this today. The Orthodox seminaries in America, even if they do not at the present moment agree with the ordination of women to the priesthood, should recognize the tradition of the female deaconate and institute plans of study for women interested in this vocation. Women are encouraged, presently, to attend these seminaries, but their liturgical training is limited to preaching, chanting, and reading. The more babies who are welcomed into churches with women deacons, the more church members will become accustomed to women in liturgical roles. The tradition of this church of the future will then, most likely, deem it necessary to ordain women as priests.

The Sunday of the Triumph of Orthodoxy, as it is called in our church, celebrates the restoration of the icons into the life of the church after the iconoclastic controversy of the eighth and ninth centuries. This restoration took more than a century to be realized. The day women will celebrate the liturgy at our altars will be another day of restoration, of restoring our shared humanity as women and men made in the image of God. The church must be a place where we can be not *what* we are (male, female, rich, poor) but *who* we are simply as humans, as developing icons revealed through the light of the Divine.

A Moment of Ritual

The church can impart this experience through ritual. But ritual, as a collective act, much like a play or a symphony, must reflect the harmony of its members. During my stay in an Eastern Orthodox monastery in West Virginia, I spent two hours three days a week with several others rolling incense, one of the monastery's most popular items shipped to churches and Orthodox Christians throughout the country. The experience impressed upon me the importance of ritual in the church. The shipping room in the monastery was located next door to the incense room through a thin wall. When parcels arrived from the monastery, as my dad's parish would confirm, the envelopes and boxes emitted a fragrant medley, even if they did not contain incense. Since the early fifth century, incense has been used in Christian worship services and is believed to carry prayers to heaven, symbolizing the permeation of heaven and earth. As the sound of prayers echo through the plumes rising into the sky, angels descend into the space of the liturgy.

Father James, a convert to Orthodoxy who moved to the monastery from Japan, spent many of his hours in the incense room. By the time the rest of us arrived in the afternoon, sticky clumps, about the size of large gummy candies, awaited each of us at our stations. We'd roll the moist incense clumps beneath our fingers like Play-Doh, forming long, even strands, which were later cut into quarter-inch pieces to dry. We all wore white aprons to protect our black monastic garb from the flour sprinkled on the counters so the incense would roll smoothly, but after ten minutes we all looked like bakers anyway. Boxes of latex gloves were set on the windowsills for those with dry hands, but I never wore them. I liked the touch of the incense on my hands. It took me a week to master how to move my hand back and forth with the right amount of pressure to create the even width of the cylinders. When I was done, Father James would sometimes pick up my tray, and when I said *arigato* to thank him, he'd grin and bow, revealing lines of gray on his black head.

As we worked, we'd alternate saying the Jesus prayer out loud: "Lord Jesus Christ, Son of God, have mercy on us." We stood facing tables that lined the walls, taking turns saying the prayer counterclockwise. Though we all repeated the same words, some placed emphasis on 'Lord,' others drew out 'Christ,' and many stressed 'Jesus.' Our mouths were covered with breathing masks guarding our lungs from the perfumed dust. When the monks standing next to me would recite the prayer, I couldn't see their lips but only hear their voices. The prayer would grow quieter as the monks at the other side of the room recited it, but soon it would be my neighbor's turn again, and I'd follow quietly underneath my breath. After he'd say the prayer twelve or so times, I'd wait for an interval of silence before he said it again, and then I'd hear my own voice echo from the powdery walls. When my voice would not answer back, but the voice of the monk to my left in its place, I'd retreat back among the silent choir.

A church community is rarely a monastery, but that should not stop us from offering spaces of stillness as well as occasions where our interaction with others flows with our own internal silence. As more and more of our waking hours are spent in front of computers, smartphones, and tablets, the responsibility will fall to the church to offer an embodied experience that congregants physiologically crave. Churches can offer opportunities "to get our hands dirty" in the creation of beauty. The church, of course, should have a technological presence, but it should also offer spaces where technology is intentionally absent: a garden, a sanctuary, a church hall, a corner for meditation.

Churches need to embrace their respective rituals and traditions. The long history of many rituals allows their reenactment to act as avenues of awareness into the timelessness of the present. Rituals, as repeated practices, perform the past in the present and connect the future with the now. Orthodox Christians, for this reason, value continuity with the past in order to access the eternal. But we must be vigilant that our rituals are in harmony with our theology, as practices can fall out of sync with theological truth (such as the exclusive ordination of men to the priesthood). Our theology and practice must be integral to each other, rather than only practice defining our policies.

Every ritual has a beginning, and churches, in my opinion, should not shy away from creating and reinstating rituals that create meaning. In the Eastern Orthodox tradition, the sacrament of Holy Eucharist is the church ritual par excellence. As a sacrament, it reenacts the breaking in of God into the world and communication of the Holy Spirit into our own body and souls, a ritual that continually needs to be respected. The entire church calendar, and the rituals and art designed around it, are designed to sanctify time itself. Every year reenacts the drama of Jesus conquering mortality through his resurrection; every day of the week is assigned a theological meaning (as "Sunday" in Russian still translates as "resurrection day"); every day of the year is a saint's day and is divided into the hours: matins, vespers, and compline as well prayers on the third, sixth, ninth, and midnight hours; and every minute is meant, ideally, to be occupied by ceaseless prayer. Only the liturgy of the sacrament of Communion can be celebrated at any hour of the day, outside the liturgical "hours," as it symbolizes a taste of a life outside of time, a true moment with God.

But every ritual can act as a conduit to God's grace. Rituals call forth the calming of our ever-firing brain waves in harmony with our own bodies and the bodies and souls around us. Ritual is a bodily dance of beauty and awe, transcendence and humanity, past and future. The rituals of the church and the leaders of these rituals must reflect our shared humanity as women and men made in the image of God. We are icons in progress, and ritual helps us move. The church of the future must continue to offer these moments of awe, harmony, and ritual enveloped in the grace of the Eternal God. The church of the future must continue to offer moments of eternity in the now.

DISCUSSION QUESTIONS

1. Where do you experience beauty in the church? How can this beauty be amplified?

2. What are the most profound spaces for human encounter in your Christian community? Is technology present or absent?

3. Are women ordained in your tradition? If yes, are you familiar with the history of how this decision was made? If not, what do you think about women's ordination?

4. What are the rituals that bring you into the presence of God?

5. How is God or the Divine portrayed in your worship space?

NOTES

1. Fyodor Dostoyevsky, *The Idiot*, trans. Richard Pevear and Larissa Volokhonsky (New York: Vintage Classics, 2003), 382.

Afterword

Moving Forward Together: Where Do We Go from Here?

KATHRYN MARY LOHRE

Bridging the Past and the Future

When I began my term as National Council of the Churches of Christ in the USA president in 2012, amid all the changes taking place in the religious landscape, the challenge before us was one of finding a way to be responsible to our legacy as churches and responsive to our ever-changing context for Christian witness. Our task was to set aside our nostalgia for the past and our anxiety about the future. In short, we needed to build a bridge between the past and the present.

Like Christians in all times and all places we desired to discern God's calling for the church today. As I thought about how to provide leadership to this process, I sought to identify sources of hope—inspiring visions for the future grounded in the practical realities of today. It was natural for me to turn to my own experience of the church and that of my peers. As those who had come of age—who had been formed as church leaders—in this new and emerging context, we had something unique to offer. I knew that many of us did not feel caught in the same tensions between nostalgia and anxiety experienced by our elders. Instead, we could offer a third way, a way of hope "for just such a time as this" (Esther 4:14). With these intentions, I reached out to discover what, precisely, were our hopes for the future of the church.

In the early days of this project, I tried very hard to discern patterns of shared experience and insight. I wanted to identify a clear, concise, and compelling vision that younger Christians could offer about what form, shape, and direction the future of the church should take. As I began to delve deeper into what we were saying and sharing with each other, I discovered that, in fact, our visions defied summary. They offered truth in divergent forms, analyzing the institutional, theological, social, and spiritual challenges of the churches today from different perspectives and offering provocative ideas for moving forward together. In other words, what I found was a panoply of visions that were markedly different, and meaningfully so.

Yearning for God's Future

In hindsight it is clear that the very goal of casting a single vision for the future was a fallacy, a symptom of the anxious culture in which I had been called to lead. The churches don't need a uniform vision, and neither does the world, for that matter. Our God-given unity is in our diversity; only a multiplicity of visions offers hope. This project seeks to provide an expression of this and an entry point into sharing our visions for the future of the church with each other and with the world around us. Though I wasn't able to discern a single vision, a crystallized nugget of hope, I was able to distill what I would call shared yearnings for the future of the church. These yearnings give shape to the trajectory of our forward motion. They help us to begin to respond to the question "Where do we go from here?"

The first yearning is for a bold, enhanced, reformed, and enlivened church *to exist*. The fate of the churches is not sealed in demographic research. We have experienced the life-giving abundance of God's gifts through the church and believe these gifts will always be necessary for the world to receive. The second yearning is for the churches *to transform* the lives of everyday Christians. Many of us have been transformed in Christian communities called and sent by the gospel of Jesus Christ. We wish for all Christians—regardless of status or social location—to have this experience and for all of us to have it more fully together as the body of Christ. The third yearning is for *imagination to take precedence* over institutionalization as we shape the future together. As young people, we believe the fullness of the churches' calling today will be revealed through imaginative, creative, and collaborative networks rather than strictly through institutions. This is not a dismissal of the institutional expressions of the churches but rather an insistence that even structures must be reinvented for a new era.

Moving Forward Together

These yearnings are not new or unique to younger Christians today. They have been sought after by generations of Christians for centuries, and they resonate with Christians *of all ages*. Yet I believe that with each generation they take on different meaning, demanding that we pursue authentic, intergenerational dialogue about them and about where we go from here. How do our formative contexts shape the ways in which we hope for the church to exist, to transform, and to thrive today? How do our different experiences as Christians shape how we see the future and what we hope, work, and strive for in and through the church?

An exploration of these and other questions is an ongoing process, a lifelong interchange. This project is but a starting point for a dialogue that has the potential to be mutually transforming—of ourselves and of the church—and by extension, of the world. Our task is to walk with one another in a visioning journey that is difficult and exhausting at times but also exhilarating and deeply enriching, and thus to discover the road to a renewed future.

We know that ultimately the future of the church belongs to

God. What does God yearn for us? How is God calling each of us, in our various capacities, and with our many gifts and skills, to serve God's church? This collection offers an opportunity to discern through each other's voices where God is calling us together in our life as Christians. What can we learn from the voices and visions presented here? What can we learn from our own voices and visions, and from those of our brothers and sisters who are often ignored or silenced? The innovations that are inspired among us are the work of the Holy Spirit. We are simply called to move forward together, one step at a time, into God's future. In doing so, we will surely embody the hope that is needed "for just such a time as this."

About the Contributors

Shantha Ready Alonso is the Field Organizing Manager at NETWORK LOBBY and serves as vice chair of the World Student Christian Federation. She received joint master's degrees in social work at Washington University in St. Louis and pastoral studies at Eden Theological Seminary (2009), and received her Bachelor of Arts in psychology and English from the University of Notre Dame (2005). She lives in Silver Spring, Maryland, and belongs to St. Camillus Franciscan multicultural parish.

Awet Andemicael is a doctoral student in theology at Yale University. Awet earned her Bachelor of Arts from Harvard University, her Master of Arts from the University of California, Irvine, and her Master of Arts in Religion from Yale Divinity School. She lives in New Rochelle, New York, and New Haven, Connecticut, and is a member of a Lutheran church.

Paul David Brown is pastor of Central United Methodist Church in Canton, North Carolina. Paul earned his Bachelor of Arts in history from Grove City College in Grove City, Pennsylvania, in 2003 and his Master of Divinity from Duke Divinity School in 2010. He lives in Canton, North Carolina, and is an ordained elder in the Western North Carolina Conference of the United Methodist Church.

Jaisy Joseph is a PhD student at Boston College with a focus in systematic theology and the history of Christian life and thought. She earned her Bachelor of Arts in psychology, religious studies, and leadership studies with a concentration in premedical studies from Austin College in Sherman, Texas, in 2009 and her Master of Divinity from Harvard Divinity School in 2012. She lives in Brighton, Massachusetts, and is an active member of the SyroMalabar Catholic Diocese of Chicago.

Jennifer T. Lancaster recently earned her PhD in religion from Temple University in Philadelphia. She serves as adjunct faculty teaching ethics at Eastern Mennonite University and Lebanon Valley College. Jennifer earned her Bachelor of Arts in religious studies from Stetson University in DeLand, Florida, in 2005 and her Master of Arts in Religion from Lancaster Theological Seminary in 2007. She lives in Lancaster, Pennsylvania, and is a member of the Presbyterian Church (USA).

Jennifer S. Leath is pastor of Campbell African Methodist Episcopal Church in Media, Pennsylvania, and holds a PhD in religious ethics and African American studies from Yale University. She is also assistant director for research for the Center on Black Church Studies, Sexual Politics, and Social Justice at Columbia University. Jennifer earned her Master of Divinity from Union Theological Seminary in 2007 and her Bachelor of Arts in social studies and African American studies from Harvard University in 2003. She was ordained an itinerant elder in the African Methodist Episcopal Church in 2007. Jennifer lives in New York City.

Kathryn Mary Lohre is director of ecumenical and interreligious relations for the Evangelical Lutheran Church in America. From 2012 to 2013 she served as twenty-sixth president of the National Council of the Churches of Christ in the USA, the youngest woman and the first Lutheran. Kathryn earned her Bachelor of Arts in psychology, religion, and women's studies from St. Olaf

College in Northfield, Minnesota in 1999, her Master of Divinity from Harvard Divinity School in 2003, and was awarded a Doctor of Divinity *honoris causa* from the Graduate Theological Foundation in 2011. She lives in Park Ridge, Illinois, and is a member of the Evangelical Lutheran Church in America.

Ian S. Mevorach is founding pastor of Common Street Community Church in Natick, Massachusetts. Ian earned his Bachelor of Arts in philosophy, with a minor in American religion, from Middlebury College in Middlebury, Vermont, in 2006 and his Master of Divinity from Boston University School of Theology (BUSTH) in 2009; he is currently ABD (all but dissertation) in a Doctor of Theology program at BUSTH in social and ecological ethics. He lives in Natick and is an ordained minister of the American Baptist Churches in the USA.

R. C. Miessler is the Congregational Resource Center Coordinator at Christian Theological Seminary in Indianapolis. He earned his Bachelor of Arts in journalism and religious studies from Franklin College in Franklin, Indiana, in 1998, his Master of Theological Studies from Christian Theological Seminary in Indianapolis in 2010, and his Master of Library Science from Indiana University in 2012. R. C. lives in Indianapolis and is an Eastern Orthodox Christian.

Alison VanBuskirk Philip is working on her Master of Divinity at Princeton Theological Seminary and is a candidate for ordination in the United Methodist Church. Previously she worked for the World Day of Prayer International Committee in New York City. She received a Bachelor of Arts in English, religion, and women's studies from the University of Delaware in 2007.

Erinn Staley is visiting lecturer at Wellesley College. Erinn earned her Bachelor of Arts in political science from Rhodes College in 2002, her Master of Divinity from Yale Divinity School in 2007, and her PhD in religious studies from Yale University in 2013. She lives in Wellesley, Massachusetts, and is a member of the Christian Church (Disciples of Christ).

Zachary Ugolnik is a doctoral student in the department of religion at Columbia University, focusing on the history of Christianity and Orthodox Christian studies. Zachary earned his Bachelor of Arts in religion and international relations from Syracuse University in Syracuse, New York, in 2004 and his Master of Theological Studies from Harvard Divinity School in 2009. He lives in New York City and is a member of the Orthodox Christian Church.